Getting A Grip On The Basic...

# SERVING
# GOD

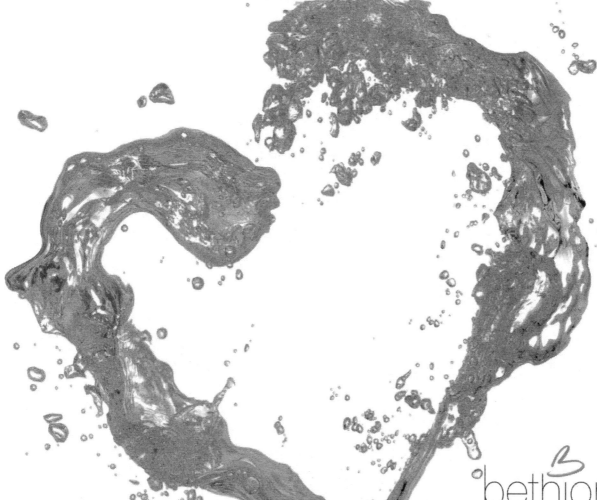

 bethjones

GETTING A GRIP ON THE BASICS
BIBLE STUDY SERIES

*Getting A Grip On The Basics of Serving God*
ISBN 13: 978-1-68031-458-8
Copyright 2002 Beth Ann Jones

Published by Jeff and Beth Jones Ministries
2500 Vincent Avenue
Kalamazoo, Michigan 49024

thebasicswithbeth.com

# CONTENTS

# ACKNOWLEDGMENTS

I would like to acknowledge the most incredible group of people I have had the privilege of knowing and serving - the staff and family of Valley Family Church. This book is the result of teaching, working, praying, laughing, crying and serving with you for the past several decades. I thank God for all of you - it's been my joy and honor to know such dedicated, servant-hearted people.

I pray the Lord uses this book fpr generations to come, to help build His Church and to train and equip church and ministry staff, leaders and volunteers who desire to hear those wonderful words, "Well done, good and faithful servant..."

May much eternal fruit that remains be the result of this study – for His glory and His kingdom purposes.

# INTRODUCTION

*"Wherefore we receiving a kingdom which cannot be moved, let us have grace,*
*whereby* **we may serve God acceptably** *with reverence and godly fear…"*
*Hebrews 12:28*

Let us have grace, so that we may serve God acceptably!

Serving God is the most exciting adventure any Christian can embark upon—it can also be very messy! That's because God has chosen to use human being to do His will and fulfill His mission on Earth and we are imperfect. We often have our own ideas, opinions, experiences and backgrounds when it comes to serving God, church life and ministry. It takes time for us to get our minds renewed to seeing and doing things the way God desires. That's the purpose of this book! When we see things from His perspective something happens in our heart and our whole view on serving the Lord, loving people and being a vital part of His Church changes. You are in for a life-changing journey as you get into God's Word to get a grip on serving God!

I am excited about what can happen in your life and the life of your church, as you study this workbook and put these principles into practice. In our experience, many pastors, leaders and church members, are looking for an easy-to-use tool for systematically training and equipping believers in their churches and ministries. I believe this book is the answer to many heart cries.

We've talked with many passionate pastors and church leaders who are sold out for reaching their communities for Christ; and yet, they often find themselves frustrated in knowing how to effectively identify, recruit, train, place and mobilize Christians into areas of service and ministry in their churches. Many times, the result is leadership and delegation by the "wing-it-and-a prayer" method. Unfortunately, this does not usually produce long-term fruit for God's Church. At the same time, there are many solid Christians and church members who want to be effective in serving the Lord, and yet because of the lack of training they have been disjointed, frustrated and ineffective as they try to serve the Lord.

Psalm 133:1-3 describes the power of a church on the same page, serving the Lord together in unity. *"Behold, how good and how pleasant it is for brethren to dwell together in unity…for there the LORD commanded the blessing, even life for evermore."* Notice that in a church where everyone is in alignment—where unity dominates—there God has commanded His blessing! We pray this book will help your church find unity by being on the same page where serving God is concerned.

**If you are a Pastor or Church Leader** – my prayer is that this workbook will serve as a tool to assist you in training and equipping your church members to join you in serving God and fulfilling the vision He has given you. I encourage you to prayerfully consider incorporating *Getting A Grip On The Basics of Serving God* into your church culture by using this workbook as a study guide for your staff, class for volunteers or in your small groups.

**If you are a Church Member** – my prayer is that this workbook provides you with a rich tour in God's Word and His plan for your life as it relates to serving Him. I pray you gain a rich revelation on how you can be the most effective in serving God and assisting your pastor and the vision of the local church you attend.

With that introduction, let's jump into our study!

# GUIDELINES FOR STUDY

## A. Guidelines for Individual Study

1. Set aside a regular time each week when you can get alone with God and study the lessons in this workbook.

2. Pray and ask the Lord to illuminate His Word to you each time you study.

3. Look up each Scripture and take time to think upon the Word of God.

4. Don't be in a hurry to complete the workbook; rather, move through the book at a steady pace and allow the Holy Spirit to minister to you personally.

## B. Guidelines for Group Study

1. No matter what size the group or class, it's important to have one leader, preferably a mature Christian, who can facilitate the group study and discussion.

2. Determine a regular time and a quiet location for the group to meet together to study the lessons in this workbook each week.

3. Pray and ask the Lord to illuminate His Word each week.

4. Look up the Scriptures and take turns reading them aloud.

5. Make each person in the group feel welcome and important; encourage each one to participate. Do not allow one person to dominate all the discussion.

6. Take time to allow for group discussion and interaction during the lessons, but avoid getting off track with side issues.

7. Don't be in a hurry to complete the workbook; rather, maintain a steady progression through the lessons and allow the Holy Spirit the freedom to minister to each individual in the group.

8. It is wise to assign the next lesson as homework each week. After the group members have done their individual study, they will be more familiar with the material. Encourage group members to write down any questions they might have and present them for discussion the next time you meet together.

# HOW TO VIEW THE BIG PICTURE

What does it mean to serve God? Why would you want to serve God? What is the purpose of serving God? How and where should you serve the Lord? What type of service does God want?

We know God doesn't want mindless robots or clones who just "do their master's bidding" out of some sort of duty or obligation; He wants sons and daughters who understand their part in His great plan and who are equipped to serve Him from a heart of love and passion! In order to serve God acceptably we need to have the big picture. We need to see things from God's perspective. We need God's vision. We need to get God's heart. Let's begin our study of the big picture by looking at a jigsaw puzzle illustration.

Have you ever put together a 1000 piece jigsaw puzzle? Do you remember how small those pieces were? Do you remember how overwhelming it seemed? What did you do first? You studied the box top, right? It's important that you have a clear understanding of what this jigsaw puzzle is supposed to look like to be successful. Perhaps the first thing you did was to begin to get specific puzzle pieces into position. Did you search for the four corner pieces first? Those four pieces are important keys to building your puzzle. The border or edge pieces are vital pieces as well. Those pieces need to be in place to effectively build your puzzle. Then the important process of connecting groups of pieces together begins, until you have enough groups to begin clumping the puzzle together. Every piece is important. One missing piece ruins the whole puzzle! Did you know there is a great parallel, in that our lives are pieces in God's big Jigsaw Puzzle? How and where do we fit? This will be our focus as we study *Getting A Grip On The Basics of Serving God.*

Imagine God has an eternal Jigsaw Puzzle with billions of pieces. Your life is a piece of God's Jigsaw Puzzle. You fit somewhere! Your life has a specific function and purpose; your life makes God's Jigsaw Puzzle complete. Jesus is the Chief corner piece! The prophets, apostles and disciples of both the old and new testaments have served as the other corner pieces and numerous border and edge pieces. Their service to God has given us the foundation and perimeter around which the Jigsaw Puzzle of God is being built. So, what about you and me; where do we fit? Likely, we are "center pieces" and by necessity we must be connected to other pieces in God's Puzzle! Your piece is vital and God's Puzzle wouldn't be the same without you! However, in order for you to be effective in finding and fulfilling your place in God's Puzzle, you need vital information. What information do you need? You need to know what the Box Top looks like! You need to study the Box Top! It's important that you have a clear understanding of what God's Jigsaw Puzzle is supposed to look like if you are to be successful in your place. Have you ever wondered what the Box Top to God's great Jigsaw Puzzle looked like? What type of picture is He developing?

God has revealed his Box Top, His big picture view in the Word. Let's look at a few foundational Scriptures regarding what the Box Top looks like.

# A. The Church is Front and Center

We are going to discover that the church is front and center on God's Jigsaw Puzzle Box Top! Did you know the Church is God's Headquarters on Earth? Everything God is doing these days on Planet Earth, He is doing in and through His Church. We'll look at God's definition of *church* in this lesson, but for now keep in mind that we are not necessarily talking about *brick and mortar* buildings, we are talking about the people who make up His church. God is not that interested in church monuments; He is interested in overseeing a church movement!

It's an exciting time to be a part of the church of the Lord Jesus Christ! Through His church, Jesus is doing marvelous things around the world. He is raising up churches with global, national, regional and local influence in every nation. Jesus loves and is building His Church!

Let's look at the value and priority God places on the church in this age.

1.   Matthew 16:18

     What did Jesus say He will do?_____

     What did Jesus say the devil will not do?_____

     Today, Jesus is focused on **building His church**. Through His church He ministers to believers and through them to the world. Notice that the enemy is fixed on fighting the church, but he won't prevail. The picture on God's Puzzle Box Top is the building of His church! It's that simple!

2.   Ephesians 5:25-27

     What type of church does God want presented?_____

     Jesus loves the church and His job is to present to himself a glorious church at His coming! Isn't that amazing? Jesus isn't coming back for a weak, divided, strife-filled, backslidden, backbiting, confused and chaotic church; He's coming back for a glorious church! We are pieces in that church!

3.   Ephesians 3:10-12

     What is God's plan for the church?_____

     In other words, Jesus is using the church to display the manifold wisdom of God to the angelic and demonic world. Imagine that!

4.   Colossians 1:18

     What is Jesus the Head of?_____

5.  Ephesians 1:22-23

What is Jesus the Head over?_____

The Message Bible paints a vivid picture of the preeminence of Jesus and His church in Ephesians 1, *"...God raised him from death and set him on a throne in deep heaven, in charge of running the universe, everything from galaxies to governments, no name and no power exempt from his rule. And not just for the time being, but forever. He is in charge of it all, has the final word on everything.* **At the center of all this, Christ rules the church.** *The church, you see is not peripheral to the world; the world is peripheral to the church. The church is Christ's body, in which he speaks and acts, by which he fills everything with his presence." (The Message)*

God's main focus during this age is the church. Building His church is the chief aim of Jesus; it's the central image on God's Jigsaw Puzzle Box Top.

Before we dive in any further, let's define our terms:

**CHURCH:** The Greek word for church in the New Testament is "ekklesia" which means "a calling out, i.e. (concretely) a popular meeting, especially a religious congregation (Jewish synagogue, or Christian community of members on earth or saints in heaven or both)."[1]

In other words, we could paraphrase by simply saying that the church is a called out group of people that gather for God's purpose. When Jesus says He will build His church, what is He saying? He is continually "calling out" those who will follow Him, who will identify with His cause and gather together for God's purpose. We see two dynamics related to the Church—there is the *global universal church* and there are *local churches*. Let's look at both of these.

**Global Universal Church of Jesus Christ:** This would include all the believers around the world who have been "called out" to become Christians—those who identify with Jesus Christ calling Him Lord and those who are in His Body. The church around the world—the global church—is made up of all types of people—people from every kindred, tribe, language, and nation that call on Jesus as Lord. (Revelation 5:9) The global universal church is made up of various denominations and groups of believers who confess Jesus as Lord, esteem His blood as the only blood of redemption, and accept the Bible as the inerrant, infallible Word of the living God.

The global universal church is being led and built by Jesus as the Head of the Church, through the Holy Spirit. He is building His church by helping each believer mature and fulfill his or her place in His Body. He is calling, anointing and appointing men and women to serve in spiritual leadership roles by His delegated authority, and He is gifting every member of the Body of Christ with various graces to serve in building up the Body. Each part must do its work! All of this is summarized in Ephesians 4:11-16, *"It was he who gave some to be apostles, some to be prophets, some to be evangelists, and some to be pastors and teachers, to prepare God's people for works of service, so that the body of Christ may be built up until we all reach unity in the faith and in the knowledge of the Son of God and become mature, attaining to the whole measure of the fullness of Christ. Then we will no longer be infants, tossed back and forth by the waves, and blown here and there by every wind of teaching and by the cunning and craftiness of men in their deceitful scheming. Instead, speaking the truth in love, we will in all things grow up into him who is the Head, that is, Christ. From him the whole body, joined and held together by every supporting ligament, grows and builds itself up in love, as each part does its work." (NIV)* The summary is that the global universal church is called to exalt

God, evangelize the world, and edify one another unto love and good works.

**The Local Church of Jesus Christ:** This would be the local representation of the global universal church in any particular town, village or city. This is a microcosm of the global church—a segment of those "called out" to follow Jesus Christ. The local church is front and center on God's priorities. It is in the local church that Christ's Body is being built up on a daily and weekly basis in millions of locations around the world. God is not the author of confusion but of decency and order, and in His Word He has established the way local churches should operate to be effective in their God-designed mission. The primary overseer in a local church is the pastor (founding, lead or senior pastor.) This person has been called by Jesus the Chief Shepherd and has been placed into an office of ministry. Depending upon its size, in addition to the God-called founding, senior or lead pastor a local church may have other pastors, administrators or leaders who assist in leadership and management. The church members (believers) are called to come along side the lead pastor and work together to fulfill the vision and function of a local church. We will see more about the flow of spiritual authority in the church in later chapters.

# B. You Have A Place In The Church

We've gotten a glimpse of the Box Top, but now we need to realize that we truly are "pieces" to God's Jigsaw Puzzle. It's vital that we understand where we fit! The good news is that you don't have to position yourself! God positions us.

1.  1 Corinthians 12:18

    What does God do for every member of the church?_____

    Jesus places us in the body of Christ, the church, as it pleases Him. He is the Head of the Church. Our job is to cooperate with His times, seasons and wisdom as He places and positions us. Our job is to understand as much as we can about His Box Top and flow with His plan as He builds His church!

2.  1 Corinthians 12:12-27

    How would you summarize the discussion in this passage on the church as a Body and each member having an

    important part?_____

    _____

3.  1 Peter 2:5

    God is building a spiritual house, His church.

    What are we called?_____

4.  Jeremiah 3:15

What does God promise He will give you?_____

5. Psalm 92:13-14

What does the Bible say about those who are planted in God's house?_____

How would you define "planted"?_____

6. Hebrews 10:25

What are we not to neglect?_____

Can you see that skipping church is a habit for some?_____

As we see the day of the Lord's return approaching, what are we to be even more diligent about? _____

Isn't it a great comfort to know that God places you in His Body, in His church as it pleases Him? He knows just where you fit! He promises to give you a pastor and spiritual leaders after His heart who will feed you. He promises that you will flourish as you are planted, committed and involved in a local church. It's God's desire that you become a faithful church attender for reasons greater than you can imagine! In future chapters, we'll discuss in more detail how you can flourish as you find and fulfill your place in God's church.

Let's summarize what we've studied so far. The church is front and center! The church is the picture that is represented on the Box Top of God's Jigsaw Puzzle. We see a detailed, three dimensional, living, moving, ever increasing, universal and local picture of the church! This is a glorious church, a church that flows with God's manifold wisdom to the degree that the spirit world knows it! We see Christ ruling the church and causing His church to be the hub of His activity on Earth. We each have part to play as God has set us in the Body as it pleased Him. This is the Box Top!

In the next chapter, let's look at how to tap into God's plan for our lives.

## C. Personal Application

Finding a local home church is vital to your success in serving God as a Christian. Unfortunately, "lone-rangers" or "spiritual vagabonds" end up on the spiritual junkheap and you don't want that to be your story. It's been said that where you attend church can be a matter of life or death. This is very true! Your eternal life, as well as the quality of life you enjoy will be largely influenced by the church you attend, the teachings you receive and the people you associate with. We encourage you to become an integral part of a local church.

1. Do You Have A Home Church?

   • If so…

      Make a determined decision to jump in and be a blessing to your Pastor and your church. Perhaps you could start by understanding the purpose, vision and mission of your church by asking yourself or your pastor these questions.

Does your church have a known purpose, vision or mission statement?_____

If so, what is it?_____

Do you understand the importance of this purpose, vision or mission?_____

If your church does not have an official vision or mission statement, how would you put into words your understanding of the purpose, vision or mission of your church?

_____

_____

- If not...

  Make a determined and prayerful decision to find a good church. The "art" of finding a good church home is simple, but it can be frustrating! Bouncing from church to church, or attending "self-appointed" home churches where there is not a God-appointed pastor is not Scriptural or healthy for you, your family or the church. It helps to know what you are looking for and what you can realistically expect from your home church.

2. Are You Looking For A Home Church?

Years ago I was introduced to these good tips for finding a home church.

**First, realize there is no perfect church!**

I am sure you already know this, but you are never going to find the "perfect" church. It doesn't exist! Churches are made up of imperfect people—so although you may not be able to find the perfect church, you can find the church that is perfect for you!

**Second, make a list of the things that are important to you.**

Ask yourself practical, spiritual questions as you visit churches:

- Does the worship of the church satisfy your heart and genuinely inspire your attention to Jesus Christ?

- Do you sense God's Presence—His life, joy, peace, love, power—in the service?

- Are the sermons based upon God's Word and relevant to the things you face in life? Do you leave the church service with an increased knowledge and awareness of God and His Word?

- Can you agree with the basic doctrines they hold to, and can you be fed spiritually at this church?

- Are there age-appropriate programs and/or activities designed for you or your family?

- Does the church offer ministry that provide opportunities for developing friendships?
- Are you challenged to grow in your own personal relationship with the Lord?

- Do you see areas of service where your gifts and talents could be utilized?

- When attending, do you "feel at home"?

### Third, look at practical considerations.

- Is the location of the church convenient enough for you to attend and be involved? If not, is it worth the drive to attend a church that meets the needs of your family? Would the inconvenient location keep you from becoming involved? Keep in mind that, where your spiritual health is concerned, the old saying, "it's worth the drive to a church that's alive" is extremely true!

- Is the schedule of services and meetings easy to integrate with your own schedule?

- Are there enough programs, classes or ministries to adequately meet the needs of everyone in your family?

### Fourth, look at important foundational requirements.

Look for a church with a strong pastor. One of the gifts that God gives to the Body of Christ is pastors. It is important to find a church with a strong pastor or husband/wife pastoral team. A strong pastor is someone who has a definite call from God to be a pastor. A strong pastor will have a loving and caring heart like Jesus did when He looked upon the multitudes and saw that they were like sheep without a shepherd. A strong pastor will have a shepherd's heart and will be a servant; his or her attitude will not be that of a dictator, but that of a servant. A strong pastor will be a leader with a vision for fulfilling what God has called his church to do. A strong pastor will teach and preach the Bible, not man's ideas, traditions or doctrines.

Look for a church that teaches and equips the believers for the work of the ministry. As a believer it is important to be a part of a church that is helping you to do the work of the ministry according to Ephesians 4:11-16. By "work of the ministry" we mean anything that has to do with building up the Body of Christ. This includes the ministry of reconciliation (soulwinning) that every believer has been entrusted with, as well as other areas of helps ministries, teaching and preaching. A good church will be teaching and equipping you so that you can function in the place that God has designed for you.

Look for a church that teaches and challenges you to grow up spiritually. It is heart-breaking to see a person who has been a Christian for a good many years but who is still a baby, spiritually speaking. A good church will speak the truth in love and challenge you to grow. At times you will need loving correction, gentle instruction and occasional reproof to help you grow into mature spiritual adulthood. A good church will challenge you to develop your own personal relationship with the Lord. This type of church will help make you a disciple of Christ, so you can develop a healthy dependence upon the Lord and His Word.

Look for a church with a loving atmosphere. There is just something about feeling "at home" in church. One of the joys of the Christian life is to be a part of a church family that loves and cares for one another. This is the type of church that edifies itself in love.

A loving church family, led by a loving pastor, will be there when needs arise in your life. Perhaps there will be a time when you will need someone to perform a marriage, a funeral, water baptism, a baby dedication, hospital visitation or pray for you or those in your family who are sick. Perhaps you will temporarily need food, clothing or material things at some time. When you are an active part of a local church, that church family will be there to help meet your needs. A church with an atmosphere of love, forgiveness and acceptance is the type of church in which you will grow and blossom.

### Fifth, visit several churches.

Take time to visit several churches. If possible, attend more than one time at each church. It takes several visits to get the heart of any organization. Attend their evening programs or small groups to get a better feel for the church. Talk to those who attend the church to find out how enthusiastic they are about the church. If possible, meet the Pastor or members of the Pastoral Staff to ask any questions you may have. After your visits, determine what you liked about each of the churches you visited and discover where your heart feels most "at home".

### Sixth, talk to the Lord.

Obviously, this is step number one as well as step number five! After you have had a chance to visit several churches, it's time to pray and seek God's will in the matter. God has a wonderful plan for your life, and according to His Word, "He sets the members in the church as it pleases Him." (1 Corinthians 12) He may very well direct you to specifically attend a given church because He knows the blessing you will receive and the blessing you will be to that particular church.

### Seventh, make a decision!

Don't wander in the "church shopping wilderness" for too long! After visiting churches and praying about it, make a decision to commit yourself to a local church. Once you make a decision to belong to a particular church, jump in with both feet! Get involved in the church. Participate in the various programs they offer for membership, new members, foundations classes and serving opportunities. Take advantage of all that the church offers to you and your family and give back to your church in your prayers, service and tithes. When you commit yourself to a church family, you'll find there is no place like home!

3.  Let's Pray

As you study through this workbook, I pray you will see just how important your church home really is! Being vitally connected to the right church, the church God has called you to at a particular season of your life, is vital to your spiritual health and well-being. Join me in praying this prayer from your heart.

### *If you are looking for a home church:*

*"Father, I thank You that Your Word tells me in Jeremiah 3:15 that You will give me Pastors after Your own heart, who will feed me with knowledge and understanding. Lord, it is my heart's desire to be in the local church You desire for me to be in at this time. Father, I desire to sit under a Pastor that has Your heart and one who will feed me Your Word and give me understanding so that I may live a life worthy of You, fully pleasing to You, and a life that bears much fruit for Your kingdom. I believe that according to Psalm 92:13 that those who are planted in the house of the LORD shall flourish, and so Father, I ask You to plant me in the church You have ordained me to be connected to so that I may flourish in every area of my life – spirit, soul, body, in relationships and in service to You. I want to serve You acceptably Lord, and I believe that it begins by involving myself in the right church and sitting under leaders after Your own heart. Father, I ask You to lead me according to Your will so that I can find and easily assimilate into my new church home. I trust You to order my steps to the church You have called me to. In Jesus' Name. Amen."*

### *If you have a home church:*

*"Father, I thank You for my church home. I thank You for giving me a Pastor/Pastors after Your heart who are feeding me with the knowledge of Your Word, and filling me with understanding so that Your Word is easy to apply in my life. I thank You for all that You are providing for me and my family through my home church and I ask You to pour out more grace, wisdom, knowledge, understanding, discernment, discretion, favor, anointing and strength on every member of my church that we may be a lighthouse for the lost, a hospital for the hurting, a buffet for the hungry and a bootcamp for being trained to serve You more effectively. I thank You Father for placing me in the Body of Christ, in my local church, as it has pleased You and I ask You to help me be a good and faithful servant in my church. In Jesus' Name. Amen."*

[1]Biblesoft's New Exhaustive Strong's Numbers and Concordance with Expanded Greek-Hebrew Dictionary. Copyright (c) 1994, Biblesoft and International Bible Translators, Inc.

# HOW TO TAP INTO GOD'S PLAN FOR YOUR LIFE

Did you know God has a great faith adventure for you? Being a true-blue, sold-out, born-again Christian is the most exciting life on Earth! He has ordained a great plan for your life! There is a destiny for you to fulfill! God wants your life to be fruitful, productive and fulfilling, and He has made provision for that to happen in your life as you walk in the light of His Word.

Jesus made it clear that God has a plan for our lives in John 15:16, *"You did not choose Me, but I chose you, and appointed you that you should go and bear fruit, and that your fruit should remain: that whatever you ask the Father in My name, He may give you."* He has chosen us! He has ordained that our lives be fruitful. Notice how Jesus describes the fruit that comes from our lives – "your fruit should remain." That means God wants us to produce good, lasting fruit!

In order for God's will to come to pass in your life, you will have to learn and cooperate with the basic principles He has established in His Word. Let's take a balanced, realistic look at how each Christian can function and fulfill their God-given destiny.

## A. God Has A Divine Plan For Your Life

1.  Jeremiah 29:11-13

    What does God know?_____

    The King James Bible says He knows the "thoughts" He thinks toward you, and the NIV Bible says He knows the "plans" He has for you.

    What type of thoughts or plans does God have for your life?_____

    What is our responsibility, according to this passage?_____

    How would you describe "seek me with all your heart"?_____

2.  Ecclesiastes 3:11

    The Amplified Bible gives a wonderful rendering of this verse:

    *"He has made everything beautiful in its time. He also has planted eternity in men's hearts and minds [a divinely implanted sense of a purpose working through the ages which nothing under the sun but God alone can satisfy], yet so that men cannot find out what God has done from the beginning to the end." (AMP)*

    How many times have you heard people, or perhaps yourself, ask the rhetorical questions, "Why am I here?" "What's my purpose?" Those questions are evidence that this passage is true!

What has God divinely implanted into the heart of every person?_____

Describe a person who has not satisfied this divinely implanted sense of purpose.

_____

Describe a person who has satisfied this divinely implanted sense of purpose.

_____

How would you describe yourself in this area?  Have you recognized and/or identified the divinely implanted sense of purpose in your life?

_____

The Bible describes God's plan for each of us in a variety of ways.  We see the terms: "good works", "fruit that remains", "race" and "course" used to describe God's plan for our lives.  Let's look at these.

3.  Ephesians 2:10

Who do we belong to?_____

What has God ordained us to walk in?_____

4.  John 15:16

Who chose you?_____

What did Jesus ordain?_____

Notice the progression in John 15:2,5,8,16 where Jesus tells us to bear fruit, then much fruit and then fruit that remains.

What do you think He is describing when He mentions "fruit that remains"?

_____

FRUIT:  What is fruit?  The Bible describes two main categories of fruit.  The fruit seen "in" our personal life with Christ and the fruit that comes "through" our personal life with Christ.  Galatians 5:22-23 describes the fruit of the Spirit that is to be seen in our personal lives.  That is, the lasting character and spiritual qualities of Jesus' image being worked in our lives.  James 5:7 describes God's longing for the fruit of souls that comes through our personal life with Christ, that is, the lasting fruit of our witness for Christ and the impact and influence we are to have in leading people to salvation through Jesus.

5.  Hebrews 12:1-2

What is set before us?_____

Who is cheering us on?_____

Each of us has a unique race to run. Our race is our destiny. We must run it by faith, and thankfully we are surrounded by a great cheering section in heaven! Jesus is the author and the finisher of our faith. He started us on this journey and He will help us to finish the race strong, as we walk in light of His Word.

6.  Acts 20:24

Paul faced some opposition as he sought to fulfill the destiny God had for his life.

How did Paul say he would finish his course?_____

The good news for every Christian is that God's will is loaded with joy! Doing God's will, fulfilling His destiny for our lives is not something we have to do with sweat, grit and a prune face! God's pathways are ways of pleasantness and peace (Proverbs 3:17) and His joy is the strength we need for fulfilling all of His will!

7.  2 Timothy 4:7

What three things did Paul declare he had done?

_____

_____

_____

God has a plan for each person. The "good works" I am called to do won't be the same as yours. The "fruit" that I am called to bring forth won't be the same as yours. The "race" that I am to run will be different than yours. The "course" I am called to finish will be unique and so will yours. The important thing is that we recognize that God has placed a "divinely implanted sense of purpose" inside each of us and it is our duty to seek the Lord and follow that plan.

The good news is that God desires for you and I to know His will. He doesn't want it to be a mystery to us. No human being can tell us what type of good works, fruit, race or course we are to fulfill. As we spend time with the Lord in prayer and in His Word, He will speak to our hearts and direct our steps.

## B. You Will Give An Account For Your Life

The Bible is full of passages that describe a coming day. A day of reckoning. A day of accountability. A day of judgment. Thank God that because of Jesus Christ, we have been washed in His blood and forgiven of all of our sins. So, we won't be judged for our sins, but we will give an account of the stewardship of our lives.  Let's look at the judgments ahead – the judgment for unbelievers and the judgment for believers.

1.    The Great White Throne Judgment For Unbelievers

   a.    Revelation 20:11-15

   Who is listed as being in attendance at The Great White Throne Judgment, according to verse 12?

   _____

   The "dead" is a reference to all those who do not believe in Jesus Christ as Lord.  This judgment is for those who do not know Jesus Christ as Lord—those who are spiritually dead and separated from God.  The Bible tells us that those who believe and receive Jesus as Lord have already passed from death to life and although they will die physically, they are not labeled as the "dead."

   What Book was opened at this judgment?_____

   This book is described in Revelation 21:27 as the Lamb's Book of Life.

   What are the "dead" judged on?_____

   All unbelievers will not have their names written in the Lamb's Book of Life and therefore they will be judged according to their works.  Since all men have sinned and fallen short of God's standard, the unbeliever's works— good and bad—will be revealed.  His bad works, or sins, will be uncovered.  Did you know this is going to be a sober moment for many people?

   According to Romans 6:23, "The wages of sin is death…" So, each unbeliever will be required to pay the wage of sin, which is eternal death in hell.  (That's why it is so wonderful to be a Christian, because Jesus has already paid our wage and we were able to go free and miss this Great White Throne Judgment and eternity in hell entirely!)  The Bible tells us that no one will be saved because of their good works; Ephesians 2:8-9 says, "For it is by grace you have been saved, through faith - and this not from yourselves, it is the gift of God - not by works, so that no one can boast." (NIV)

   The Bible goes on to tell us that if we have just one sin, it's one too many.  James 2:10 tell us that, "For whosoever shall keep the whole law, and yet offend in one point, he is guilty of all."  Can you imagine being the nicest person on Earth, who just sinned once?  Can you imagine how your countenance would fall when you found out that the wages of that one sin was still death?  Galatians 2:21 tells us that if we could obtain right standing with God through our good works, then Christ died in vain.

   b.    Who's Who In Hell - Revelation 21:8, Galatians 5:19-21, 1 Corinthians 6:9-11, Romans 1:18-2:1

   Look at these verses and list those who will not enter God's kingdom, but who will spend their eternity in hell.

The Great White Throne Judgment is going to be a terribly sad awakening for many unbelievers, and unfortunately for them it will be too late to change their minds. For the Christian, because we believe and have received the work that Jesus did in dying for our sins and taking the punishment that we deserved, our names have been written in the Lamb's Book of Life and we will never face the Great White Throne Judgment.

However, each Christian does have a judgment to face: it's called The Judgment Seat of Christ, where our works will be judged and rewards will be given based upon those works. Let's look at this judgment for believers.

2.   The Judgment Seat of Christ For Believers

   a.   We Will All Stand Before The Judgment Seat of Christ

   Romans 14:10

   What will all Christian brothers and sisters stand before?_____

   2 Corinthians 5:10

   What will all believers stand before?_____

   What will happen at the judgment seat of Christ? Let's look at the things we, as believers, will be judged on.

   b.   We Will Be Judged On How We Lived Our Lives

   1 Corinthians 3:10-15

   We are told to take heed to how we build upon the foundation of Jesus Christ in our lives. We can build with two sets of materials; describe these two sets:

   _____ or _____

   _____ or _____

   _____ or _____

   How will God test the material quality of our lives?_____

   What happens to wood, hay and stubble in fire?_____

   What happens to gold, silver, and precious stones in fire?_____

   What do you understand the wood, hay, stubble and/or the gold, silver and precious stones to represent?

_____

Describe the way God will reward believers._____

What are you building with in your life?_____

c.    We Will Be Judged On The Words We Spoke

Matthew 12:36-37

What did Jesus say we would give an account of?_____

We are going to be justified or condemned by our words.  What do you think this means?


_____

Jesus had so much to say about words and the power of what we say.  The book of Proverbs tells us that the power of life and death is in the tongue.  James tells us that our tongue gives direction to our lives in the same way that a rudder directs a ship or a bridle is used to direct a horse.  There is tremendous power in our mouths! In fact, if we were honest, we could look at our lives and the fruit of our lives and we would see that our lot in life is a direct reflection of the words we have spoken.  We are eating the fruit of our lips—just like Proverbs 18:20-21 says!

d.    We Will Be Judged On How We Handled God's Word

2 Timothy 2:15

What are we told to do with God's Word?_____

What would cause a person to be disapproved by God?_____

How much control do we have over being ashamed or approved?_____

How are we to divide or handle the Word?_____

We are challenged to "rightly divide" the Word, which implies that it can be wrongly divided.  We are told to handle God's Word correctly, which implies that it can be wrongly handled.  We will be held accountable for our handling of God's Word.

e.    We Will Be Judged On The Motives Of Our Heart

1 Corinthians 4:5

What will God reveal about our hearts?_____

As believers, it's an important heart decision to choose to live according to God's Word and to glorify Him with our lives. We will give an account of our lives someday. Let's talk about living in light of eternity.

## C. Choose To Live Your Life From The Eternal Perspective

1.  2 Corinthians 4:17-18

List as many things as you can think of that are temporal. _____

_____

List as many things as you can think of that are eternal. _____

_____

What are you spending most of your time investing in – temporal or the eternal things? _____

One of the most powerful illustrations I heard as a young Christian, and one that literally changed my life, is what I have called "the dot/line" question. Let me share it with you.

Look at the "line" below and let it represent eternity. Put arrows on either end of this line to show that it goes in both directions for eternity. Somewhere on the line draw a "dot" and let that represent your temporary life. The "dot" will represent your 70, 80, 90 or 100 years of life on planet Earth.

_____

The question to ask yourself is this: "Am I living for the 'dot' or the 'line'?" In other words, are you living for eternal things or temporal things? Are you building on the foundation of Jesus Christ in your life using eternal materials like gold, silver and precious stones, or are you building with temporal things like wood, hay and stubble? Did you know that if you choose to live your "dot" for the "line" you can literally invest your lifetime into eternal things and the result will be that your life's impact outlives you?! Your "dot" can live for the "line" by giving your life to eternal things like God, Jesus, God's Word, and the salvation and eternal destination of people! I challenge you to make a decision to use your "dot" so that it affects the "line"!

## D. Application

Is your heart stirred? Does something deep inside of you long to know and fulfill all of God's will? Do you want to make a quality decision to live for eternal things—to fulfill the divinely implanted sense of purpose that God's placed inside of you? Here is a great pattern for praying this very thing into your life! One of the Apostle Paul's friends, Epaphras, prayed this prayer for the Christians in Colossians 4:12, "Epaphras, who is one of you and a servant of Christ Jesus, sends greetings. He is always wrestling in prayer for you, that you may stand firm in all the will of God, mature and fully assured." (NIV) Why not join me in praying this prayer for you!

*"Dear Heavenly Father, we thank You that You know the plans You have for us and they are good plans. We thank You Father for the divinely implanted sense of purpose You've placed in us. It's our heart's desire to fulfill Your plan and destiny for our lives, to do the good works, bear the fruit, run the race and finish the course You've ordained for us. Father, we choose this day to live for You and Your purposes – to live our temporary dots for the eternal line. Father, we ask that You would give us the grace we need to stand perfect and complete in all Your will. Thank you Holy Spirit for being our Helper in these things. In Jesus' Name. Amen"*

# CHAPTER 3

# HOW TO LOSE YOUR LIFE

Did you know that you are not your own? You don't belong to yourself! You gave up your right to yourself when you confessed Jesus as Lord! As a Christian, you've been purchased by Someone else. Did you know there is a "sold" sign on you? You belong to God. You are His property! Jesus Christ purchased you with His very own blood. He paid the ultimate price so that you could belong to God. When you confessed Jesus as your Lord, you gave up the right to yourself. It's a fact that many Christians have not realized! Many Christians still live their lives, make their choices, do their thing as if God did not own them. They act like they own themselves! Have you ever really thought about it? Have you considered the ramifications of being purchased by God and not owning yourself?

For example, if you own a car, you are in charge of that car, right? You direct the car where to go. You determine what type of fuel to put in the car. You are the owner and you get to call the shots. What if someone else purchased your car; who would get to direct the car? If someone else owned your car, would you still be able to take that car anywhere you wanted? No, of course not. Once you give up the ownership of that car, it belongs to a new owner and that person gets to be in charge of the future and destiny of that car. Did you know the same is true where our relationship with the Lord is concerned? We've been purchased by God and we are not our own, He now legally gets to direct the future and destiny of our lives. However, it's vital that we give up our right to ourselves; that we lose our life!

Let's look at this subject:

## A. You Belong To God

1.  1 Corinthians 6:19-20

    Who lives in your body?_____

    What does the phrase, "you are not your own" mean to you?_____

    _____

    Who bought you and what was the price?_____

    We are to glorify God in two areas of our life, what two areas?

    _____        _____

    Who owns our spirit and our body?_____

2.   1 Corinthians 7:23

Define the phrase, "you were bought" in your own words.

_____

3.   2 Timothy 2:19-21

What does the Lord know?_____

What are the two types of vessels or articles that are described?

_____          _____

To be useful to God as a vessel of honor, what must we do?_____

# B. You Must Consider Yourself Dead

Did you know before we can really live for God, we must realize that we are dead?  We need to recognize that we've been crucified with Christ and there is a "law of death and resurrection" that will operate throughout our Christian lives.

1.   Galatians 2:20

What happened to you when Jesus was crucified?_____

You are still alive, but not in the same way.  Describe your life according to this verse.

_____

2.   2 Corinthians 5:17

Any person who is "in Christ" is called what?_____

What happened to the "old you"?_____

3.   John 12:24-26

What has to happen to a grain of corn before it can germinate and bring forth fruit?

_____

What has to happen to our lives before it can bring forth fruit?

_____

4.  Romans 12:1

    While we are alive, we are to present our lives to God in what fashion?

    _____

5.  Mark 8:34-38

    What three things did Jesus say we must do?

    _____

    _____

    _____

    If we refuse to lose our lives, what is the result?_____

    If we lose our life, what is the result?_____

6.  Romans 6:11-15

    What are we to be dead to?_____

    Who are we to be alive to?_____

    What are we not to yield our flesh/bodies to?_____

    Who are we to yield our flesh/bodies to?_____

## C. You'll Have To Say Goodbye

As a sincere Christian, there are some things you'll have to say goodbye to if you want to live the genuine, fruitful Christian life. Let's look at several of these.

1.  Goodbye To Selfish Ambition

    a.  John 5:30

        Jesus was the Master at denying His own ambition. Look at this verse from the Amplified Bible.

        *"I am able to do nothing from Myself [independently, of My own accord—but only as I am taught by God and as I get His orders.] Even as I hear, I judge [I decide as I am bidden to decide. As the voice comes to Me, so I*

*give a decision], and My judgment is right (just, righteous), because I do not seek or consult My own will [I have no desire to do what is pleasing to Myself, My own aim, My own purpose] but only the will and pleasure of the Father Who sent me." (AMP)*

What did Jesus say He did?_____

Jesus had no desire to do what?_____

What did Jesus not even consult?_____

b.  Luke 22:42

Whose will did Jesus choose?_____

We see Jesus praying the prayer of consecration in this passage. He was consecrating His life to the will of God the Father. If Jesus had chosen what He wanted, He may not have gone to the cross. He said, "not my will" indicating that His will had to submit to God's will. He had to give up His desire and ambition and submit to God's plan for His life. We will have to do the same thing at times. We will have to submit what we want to do, to God. We will have to say, "not my will Father, but Yours be done."

2.  Goodbye To Confidence In The Flesh

a.  Philippians 3:3-4

What are we to have no confidence in?_____

b.  Proverbs 3:26

What is our confidence supposed to be in?_____

c.  John 15:5

What can we do apart from Christ?_____

d.  Philippians 4:13

What can we do through Christ?_____

This can be a difficult lesson to learn, especially if we have leaned heavily on our own energy, efforts, talents, personality or skills. We must realize that apart from Christ we can do nothing, yet through Christ we can do all things.

3.  Goodbye to Human Praise

    a.  John 12:43

        What should we be most interested in?_____

        Don't get in a ditch here. It's nice to receive a compliment from others, and you should not be uncomfortable when people speak kind and edifying words to you, however, you just don't want to crave or require those words! We need to seek God's approval and praise, even if no one else approves or compliments us.

    b.  Hebrews 6:10

        What does God keep good records of?_____

4.  Goodbye to Self Promotion

    a.  John 7:16-18

        When we constantly speak of ourselves, what are we really seeking?_____

    b.  Proverbs 27:2

        Who should praise or compliment us?_____

        Who shouldn't praise or compliment us?_____

    c.  Luke 12:16-21

        How many times did this man use the word "I" or "my" in this story?_____

        We need to be watchful, yet not paranoid, over how much we speak of ourselves, and the motive for doing so. Are we boasting? Are we talking about ourselves constantly? Are we trying to impress someone? Are we "tooting our own horn"? Don't be the kind of person that is always talking about "you"! To check up on yourself, the next time you are sharing listen to what you are saying and see how many times the word "I" is used! We need to be sure that God is getting the glory and credit in our lives. On the other hand, many times it is appropriate to speak of what God has done in your life and to share your testimony or a particular story of God's faithfulness in your life. By recounting these things you are encouraged as you see what the Lord has done in your life, He gets the glory and the credit, you receive the benefit, and those who hear your story are encouraged or taught.

To serve God effectively, we must come to the place where we are dead to sin, to our own plans, to our own ambitions, and to our own desires and yet, we are to be very much alive to God and His righteousness, plans, ambitions and desires for our lives. As Christians we must say "goodbye" to some things in order to say "hello" to things God has prepared. We must come to understand that this "law of death and resurrection" is a kingdom principle we must cooperate with to be effective in serving God.

Are you ready to consecrate your life to God afresh? Perhaps you've dedicated your life to God before, but it would be good for your heart to consecrate afresh. We can pray a simple prayer together.

*"Father, I choose to submit my life and my will to Your will. I give up my rights to myself and I recognize that I was bought with a price. I belong to You. I am Yours. Jesus, be the Lord of my life. I give myself completely to You. I dedicate and consecrate myself to You and Your will. Help me to live a life pleasing to You with no regrets. I will do what You want me to do. I will say what You want me to say. I will go where You want me to go. Father, I ask You to lead me and guide me that I may stand perfect and complete in all of Your will. In Jesus' Name. Amen."*

## D. Application

Can you think of a time or season in your life when you learned by experience the reality of John 15:5 and Philippians 4:13? Have you learned in truth that apart from Christ you can do nothing and yet through Christ you can do all things? It sounds like an oxymoron, doesn't it? However, in areas of our life where we are putting our confidence in the flesh, it seems that we have to learn the lesson of realizing that we can't do anything apart from Christ—that literally our "self-confidence" dies and we recognize our utter dependence upon Him for anything fruitful to result in our lives. This is a most difficult lesson. Right on the heels of experiencing John 15:5 in our lives, it seems that the Lord then takes us to Philippians 4:13 and instills in us the great truth that through Christ we can do all things. He empowers us to do the very things we realized that we could not do apart from Him!

It seems that anyone in the Bible who was used by God in a significant way had to learn the lesson of losing their life.

Think of Moses. Realizing the call of God in his life, he stepped out prematurely in his own efforts to deliver the Israelites from Egyptian bondage. Moses had to learn that lesson of putting no confidence in the flesh, and for 40 years he lived on the backside of the desert losing his life! It is interesting that just about the time Moses felt like a useless stutterer, God came on the scene to revive the call on his life. God spoke to Moses out of a burning bush and instilled the confidence that through God's power, Moses could deliver the Israelites. It took over 40 years, but look at the supernatural fruit of Moses' life. (Exodus 2-4)

Think of Paul. Paul was a smart, well-connected, highly religious guy! God called him to preach the very gospel he had opposed. God had big plans for Paul, but before he could be used by God, Paul would have to learn that apart from Christ he could do nothing. Paul suffered great persecution to preach the gospel. He lost his life and counted it rubbish in order to know and serve the Lord. Paul lost his life and was empowered to do all things God had called him to do through Christ. (Philippians 3:7-14)

Think of Jesus Himself. Jesus had to humble himself and become a man, a human being. He chose to make himself of no reputation, but took on the form of a servant. He chose to lose His life on our behalf and therefore God was able to highly exalt Him and give Him the Name above every name in heaven, on Earth and under the Earth. The fruit of Jesus' life continues to this day! We are the fruit of His life! (Philippians 2:5-11)

Have you lost your life? Have you experienced the reality of knowing that apart from Christ you can do nothing? Describe this in your life.

Have you realized that through Christ you can do all the things He has called you to do?

---

# HOW TO BE GREAT IN GOD'S KINGDOM

When you think of great people, who comes to your mind? What qualities make them great in your thinking? Is it their Christianity? Is it their relationship with the Lord? Is it their character? Is it their accomplishments? Is it their influence? Is it their wealth? Is it their generosity? Speaking ability? Creativity? Kindness? Wisdom? What makes a person great in God's eyes?

One day several of Jesus' disciples were arguing about this very thing. They were disputing among themselves as to who was the greatest among them. They were vying for the top spot on God's list! The most interesting thing is Jesus' response. He did not rebuke them for their desire to be great. He did not scold them for such an unrighteous desire. Rather, He defined greatness. Let's look at it.

## A. If You Want To Be Great In God's Kingdom

1.   Matthew 23:11

     To be the greatest in God's kingdom, what must we become?_____

2.   Matthew 20:26,27

     If we want to be great in God's kingdom, what must we do?_____

3.   Matthew 18:1-4

     Who is the greatest in God's kingdom?_____

4.   Mark 9:33-35

     To be first and great, what must we do?_____

     To be recognized as great in God's kingdom we must be humble servants of all.

## B. If You Want To Hear "Well Done, Good And Faithful Servant"

The Lord has given to each one of us a variety of things over which we are to be good stewards. We are stewards over our life, our time, our talents, our material resources and our money. God is expecting us to use all of those things in our service to and for Him. Let's look at this:

1.   Matthew 25:14-29

In this passage we see Jesus expects a return on the talents He has given.

What did the Lord say about those who were good stewards of their talents?

_____

What did the Lord say to the servant who was a bad steward of his talent?

_____

2.   1 Peter 4:10

Who has received gifts?_____

What are we to do with the gifts we have received?_____

Perhaps you wonder what specific things God has given you stewardship over.  What gifts and talents has He given you?  Each of us is to be a good steward with our time, talents and tithe.  To help you evaluate your stewardship, answer these questions:

a.   YOUR THOUGHTS:  What do you spend the majority of your time thinking about?_____

_____

b.   YOUR TIME:  How do you spend your time?_____

c.   YOUR GIFTS:  What gifts, talents or abilities has the Lord given you?

_____

d.   YOUR SERVICE:  To what extent are you using those gifts for His glory – whether in your vocation or your church involvement – in whatever capacity you are serving Him?

_____

e.   YOUR MONEY:  How do you spend your money?  What percentage of your finances are you giving away, in tithes to your local church and in offerings or alms to bless others?

_____

f.   YOUR RELATIONSHIPS:  How do you treat the people God has placed in your life?  At home?  At work?  In social settings?  At church?

_____

g.  YOUR BODY:  How well are taking care of the body the Lord gave you?

_____

# C. If You Want God To Promote You

Did you know there is an acid test you must pass to receive God's promotion?  Sure, you can promote yourself if you want to.  You can find yourself in self-appointed positions, too.  But, it's empty and God is not in it.  So, how do you put yourself in a position for God to promote you in His service?  There is one big test you must pass!  It's the faithfulness test!  Unfortunately, this is a test that many Christians flunk and have to take again and again. Let's discuss it.

1.  1 Timothy 1:12

    What is God looking for; what is He counting or considering?_____

    When God counts us faithful, what does He do?_____

    God is watching our faithfulness, and when He counts us faithful He puts us in the ministry; He promotes us to His service.

2.  1 Corinthians 4:1-2

    How should people regard us?_____

    What is required of God's stewards?_____

3.  Luke 16:10-12

    Faithfulness begins with the small things.  Faithfulness begins with caring about other people's things.

    What does this say about a person who is faithful in little things?_____

    What does this say about a person who is unfaithful in little things?_____

    Jesus contrasts our faithfulness with money to our faithfulness with spiritual truths.  What is His point?_____

    _____

    If we are faithful in another person's organization, business, church or vision, what will God give us?

    _____

4.  2 Timothy 2:2

    What type of people can be entrusted with spiritual truths they can then pass on to others?

    _____

5.  Proverbs 28:20

    What happens to a faithful person?_____

Can you see the value God places on faithfulness? He's watching. It's being faithful in little things that makes a big difference. In serving God, faithfulness becomes practical in things like how you take care of the natural things—your body, your home, your car, your possessions. Did you know that sloppy people are rarely faithful? Being faithful becomes practical in how you take care of other people's things, too. It is reflected in how you relate to your family and friends through your attitudes, your words, your commitment to fairness and to their best interests. Being faithful becomes practical in how you fulfill the service and leadership roles you've been assigned—being a person of your word, showing up when you say you will, fulfilling commitments you make, doing the tasks you've been given with excellence, keeping a good attitude, guarding your mouth and allowing the Word to be your standard. These are all practical areas of faithfulness. When we pass the faithfulness test—when God counts us faithful—He promotes us!

# D. Application

Let's talk about very practical areas of life. Habits. Attitudes. Associations. Lifestyles. Did you know that these things are important? The habits you develop—what you eat, drink, smoke, and say—will either glorify God or they won't. The type of people you associate with will affect you in either a positive, godly way or in a negative, ungodly way. Your lifestyle—places you frequent, videos you watch, music you listen to, internet sites you visit—these are all indicators of your heart condition. Your sexual identity and purity matter. Do your habits, associations and lifestyle choices glorify God? Is it your heart's desire to overcome any stronghold that may have a grip in your life, so that you may glorify God in your entire life?

Did you know that as you increase in your service to God and in your leadership roles you lose options? By becoming a servant to all, you lose the option to let your flesh dominate your life, to have temper tantrums, to have pity parties, to have fits of jealousy, to make excuses for ungodly habits and to live a carnal, undisciplined life. Growing in your service to God means that you also lose your right to hold onto certain habits and lifestyles. God loves you, but as you mature and serve Him with your life, He expects you to grow up and to live a truly dedicated life. Let's look at this very practical subject.

We live in a permissive and promiscuous society where people often times justify behavior in relative terms, rather than living by God's Word and His absolutes. In the Christian and church world, as people are born-again and begin growing in their walk and service to God, they often find the areas of drinking, smoking, bad language, off-color jokes, immorality, premarital or extramarital sex, divorce and remarriage, gambling, movie and video choices, music preferences and the like become real heart issues that must be addressed. If you are dealing with any of these areas and struggling in any way, I encourage you to seek the Lord and take His Word to heart. He will help you to follow and obey His will. If you need extra support and guidance, I encourage you to speak with your Pastor or a mature believer for guidance and encouragement. Let's look at several verses of Scripture which speak to these subjects in a general way.

1.  1 Corinthians 6:12; 10:23-24

    What do these verses describe?_____

2.  Colossians 1:10, 1 Thessalonians 2:12

    What type of life are we supposed to live?_____

3.  1 Corinthians 10:31

    What are we supposed to do in our eating, drinking and in all we do?

    _____

4.  1 Thessalonians 5:22

    What are we to avoid?_____

5.  Psalms 101

    How did the writer say he would live in his home?_____

    What would he not set before his eyes?_____

    What type of people would he not associate with?_____

6.  Romans 14:21

    What should we do so that we don't cause our fellow Christian to stumble?

    _____

7.  Luke 21:34, Romans 13:13, Galatians 5:19-21, 1 Peter 4:2-5, Proverbs 31:4-6

    What do these verses say about getting drunk?_____

    How do these verses describe God's view of ungodly partying?_____

    While people debate whether Jesus turned the water at the wedding in Cana into real, alcoholic wine, it is clear that Jesus and the whole of Scripture clearly teach against drunkenness and living the ungoldy, immoral party life.

8.  1 Corithians 6:18, Ephesians 5:3-5, 1 Thessalonians 4:3-7

    What does God say about sleeping around and sexual relations outside of marriage?

    _____

9.  Romans 1:21-32, 1 Corinthians 6:9-11

    How do these passages describe God's view of homosexuality?_____

    _____

10. Romans 13:14, 2 Timothy 2:22, Jude 16-19

    What does the Bible say about lust—pornography and perversion?_____

    _____

God loves everyone, sinner and saint alike! He loves the fornicator, the adulterer, the porn addict and the sexually immoral and yet He has given us His will concerning our sexuality in His Word. If we want to walk in God's blessings, we must make the choice to resist any and all sexual temptations and align our lives with His Word.

Maybe this would be a good time to evaluate your habits, attitudes, lifestyle, associations and perhaps repent. Are you willing to consecrate your entire life, spirit, soul and body to the Lordship of Jesus and His Word? As you think about your heart and actions in the area of being a servant, a good steward and a faithful person, do you see room for improvement? Why not pray a prayer like this from your heart and write down the actions and adjustments you plan to make.

*"Dear Father God, I am so thankful that I can come boldly to Your throne of grace to obtain mercy and find grace to help me in my time of need. I recognize the areas of my life where I have sinned, where I have not followed Your will, where I have displeased You and I repent and turn 180 degrees from: (list the area or areas that God has dealt with your heart)_____. I ask You to forgive me and to cleanse me from all unrighteousness and I ask You for Your grace to help me walk in a manner worthy of You, fully pleasing to You. Thank You Father for Your forgiveness and Your grace to help. In Jesus' Name. Amen."*

If you are looking for additional support and help, we encourage you to talk to your pastor, Christian counselors, therapists or other mature believers who can give you the support you need.

# HOW TO FIND YOUR PLACE

How do you practically find your place in God's kingdom? How do you flow with God's plan for your life? Where do you begin? As a born-again believer who is filled with the Holy Spirit, growing in your faith and consecrated to God's will, where do you start serving? First base in ministry is what the Bible calls, "the ministry of helps". You can begin by simply starting to "help" in and through your local church.

As a new believer, with a hunger for knowing and serving God, I remember being frustrated by not knowing where to begin. What do I do with the zeal? What do I do with the passion? What do I do when I am green and inexperienced? How could I find my place? I remember asking an older, more mature Christian what I should do. She gave me a golden nugget. This woman simply said, "Begin serving God in your local church and God will promote you from there." It seemed so simple. It seemed so unspectacular! It almost seemed boring, but it is God's vehicle for finding our place in His plan.

Let's look at the practical dimensions of serving God in our local church and let's examine some of the mistakes and ditches we want to avoid in this process.

## A. Your Place Begins By Helping

The best way to find your place in God's plan is to start helping! Help your family and friends. Help your boss. Help your church. The Bible describes a very important ministry—the starting place for everyone who wants to serve God well. It's called: the ministry of helps. Let's look at it.

1.  The Ministry of Helps Defined

    The Bible lists "the ministry of helps" as a valid ministry. Let's define our terms:

    MINISTRY: The Greek word for ministry is "diakonia", which means attendance (as a servant, etc.) and can also be translated as administer, minister, ministry, office, relief or service. The ministry is simply service that brings relief![1]

    HELPS: The Greek word for help is "antilepsis" which simply means relief, aid or help. The ministry of helps is a great relief to church leaders and a tremendous aid or help to any ministry![2]

    a.  Romans 8:26

        The first and best Helper is who?_____

    b.  1 Corinthians 12:28

        Do you see the "helps" ministry in 1 Corinthians 12:28?_____

The helps ministry is a starting point for most believers. Let's say a believer is called by God to eventually serve in the office of a Pastor; their first place of service will likely be in the helps ministry where they can demonstrate faithfulness and allow their gift to make a way for them.

For others the ministry of helps is the starting and finishing point. The helps ministry is an office that some (and in fact, most) believers are called to fulfill as their unique calling and final destination in the body of Christ—the ministry of helps is their place! We should never underestimate or under-esteem the importance and power of believers who function in the ministry of helps to move God's plan forward!

2.  Old Testament Examples of The Ministry of Helps

    a.  Genesis 2:18-20

    God demonstrated the power of the ministry of helps in the marriage relation.  What is one ministry of every wife?

    _____

    b.  1 Chronicles 12:1, 17-22

    We see the tremendous power of the ministry of helps in the life and ministry of David.  Because of the mighty men that came to help David, he was able to stand in the appointed place God had anointed him for as King.

    In verse 1, what are David's mighty men called?_____

    In verse 17, we realize that David had been betrayed numerous times, and he was looking for genuine helpers whose hearts would be knit to his heart.  What was Amasia's response to David?

    _____

    In verse 21, what did David's helpers do?_____

    In verse 22, we see that God had touched many hearts to help David.  Describe his helpers.

    _____

    c.  Exodus 31:2-6; 35:30-36:2

    God had called by name two men to help Moses.  They were handpicked, gifted, skilled and anointed to help fulfill God's plan and the vision God had given to Moses.  Let's look at this story:

    In verse 2 and verse 6, what are the names of the two helpers God raised up to assist Moses?

    _____          _____

How had God equipped Bezaleel and Aholiab, according to verses 31:3-5; 35:31-36:1?

_____

d.  Exodus 17:9-12

When Israel faced a battle, Moses received a strategy from God for defeating the Amalekites.  As Moses held up his hands, Israel prevailed in battle, but when he let his hands down, Amalek prevailed.  Moses needed help holding his hands up.  Who were his helpers?

_____        _____

How important was the "ministry of helps" in this case?_____

Can you see the importance of "helping" to hold up the hands of those you serve under?

_____

e.  1 Samuel 14:7-17; 16:21; 31:4-6

The Old Testament describes the ministry of helps as that of the "armorbearer".  Read these passages and see if you can identify the heart of the armorbearer.  Describe an armorbearer in your own words.  Describe the relationship between the armourbearer and the one he/she is serving.

_____

_____

3.  New Testament Examples of the Ministry of Helps

a.  Luke 5:3-9

Look at the power of the ministry of helps to "catch fish".  Imagine how much more powerful the outreach of a local church could be if there were more helpers with the right heart.

Jesus knew where the fish were.  What did He tell Simon Peter?

_____

By obeying Jesus, what did Peter receive?_____

In verse 7, what was necessary for them to bring in the net-breaking, boat-sinking load of fish?

_____

Can you see that it is going to take lots of helpers in the church to reap the great harvest in every city?

_____

b.   Acts 6:1-7

One of the best New Testament examples of the ministry of helps in a growing ministry is described in Acts 6.

When a ministry grows and multiplies there can often be challenges.  Describe the challenge in verse 1.

_____

The leaders realized that they needed helpers.  They decided to choose seven people to serve in this helps ministry.  What were the qualifications for these seven people?

_____

_____

The leaders needed to keep their priorities in place, and focus on the things that God had called and appointed them to do.  What was the focus of the church leaders supposed to be?

_____

Notice the result of this wise decision in verse 5 and 7.  What was the result?

_____

c.   Acts 16:9

God thinks the ministry of helps is important.  He gave Paul a vision of the people of Macedonia's need for help in this passage – they needed the gospel of Jesus.

What did Paul see in the vision?_____

d.   Romans 16:3-4

Who were Priscilla and Aquila?_____

Describe how they helped Paul._____

e.   Acts 18:24-28

Apollos was a mighty man in the Scriptures and quite gifted in speaking, teaching and explaining that Jesus was the Christ. Through his teaching and speaking gift he was a big help. What characteristics describe this man in the ministry of helps?

_____

f.    1 Corinthians 16:15-18

Paul describes his friends in ministry that had addicted themselves to the ministry of the saints.

How did the ministry of Stephanas bless Paul?_____

4.    The Role of Elders and Deacons And The Ministry of Helps

How do elders and deacons fit into the ministry of a local church? There are a variety of ways that elders and deacons are incorporated into any church government structure. There are different schools of thought on church government and spiritual oversight. In some churches that function under a Pastor-led form of church government, elders or elder board, deacons or deacon board are appointed to assist the Pastor. In other churches, the elders or deacons may be staff members that the Pastor has appointed to assist him. In some churches, the elders and/or deacons are voted in by the congregation to oversee the affairs of the church—either the spiritual, business and/or legal matters while the Pastor is accountable to fulfill the assignments he is given by them. There are many varieties of church government and in this workbook we will not tackle the pros and cons of church government styles, but we will look at a few general truths of Scripture to identify the "helps" component of elders and deacons. In general, elders help with spiritual oversight while deacons help with natural, practical affairs of the church. What do these verses tell us?

a.    Acts 6:1-7

In what way did these deacons assist the leaders of the early Church?

_____

b.    1 Timothy 3:1-15

Describe some of the qualifications listed for bishops and deacons. Notice that people with these character traits would be a great help in a local church!

_____

_____

## B. Your Place Includes The Ministry Of Excellence

Being a servant for God means doing everything with excellence.  God is not impressed by sloppy, half-hearted service.  We are to honor God not only with what we do, but how we do it.  Let's look at the power of excellence.

1.    God Wants Us To Have An Excellent Spirit

    a.    Daniel 5:12,14; 6:3

        How was Daniel known?_____

    b.    Proverbs 17:27

        What does a man of understanding have?_____

2.    God Wants Us To Do Things With Excellence

    a.    1 Corinthians 12:31; 13:1-8

        What is God's most excellent way?_____

    b.    1 Kings 10:1-8

        The queen of Sheba had heard of the fame of Solomon and the God he served. She traveled to Jerusalem to visit him, arriving with quite an entourage.  One thing nearly took her breath away and that was the excellence of Solomon's helps ministers.  Let's look at this:

        In verse 5, describe the excellence of the food that was served._____

        If you are gifted to cook and provide food service, make sure every dish is prepared and served with excellence.

        Describe the disposition of Solomon's servants._____

        If you are serving in the ministry of helps, be sure your attitude and conduct befits someone serving the King of kings!

        Describe their apparel._____

        If you are serving in the ministry of helps, be aware that your apparel and appearance does matter.  Dress and grooming are first impressions and many times these things will give you access or deny you access to someone's heart.

        Describe the way Solomon carried himself._____

Did you know that the way you carry yourself will send a message?  A message of excellence, sloppiness, arrogance, humility, godliness, worldliness, success or failure can be identified many times by the way people carry themselves. Describe how the spirit of excellence the queen witnessed among Solomon's helps ministry (vv. 6-8) affected her.  What did she say?

_____

How did she describe those who served in helps ministry?

_____

## C. Your Place Will Flourish As Your Gift Makes A Way

You've heard the phrase, "use it or lose it"?  It's vital that you use the gift or gifts God has given you, and as you do His grace will be evident in your life.  Your gift may not be recognized or correctly discerned by you or others at first.  There may then be a season of "practicing" and "experimenting" to find the right fit in the right season for your gift or gifts to be maximized, but in that right time and right place your gift will make a way for you.  Let's look at this:

1.  Proverbs 17:8

    A gift is precious and we should esteem any gifts that the Lord has given us.  According to this verse, what does this gift do as it begins to be used?

    _____

2.  Proverbs 18:16

    What does a person's gift do for him as it is employed?_____

3.  1 Timothy 4:14-5:1

    What are we to do with the gifts we've been given?_____

    _____

4.  2 Timothy 1:6

    What are we to do with the gifts we've been given according to this verse?

    _____

STIR UP:  The idea here is to "fan the flame"!  To stoke the embers on the inside of you!  In other words, there are times you may not "feel" motivated to serve the Lord with the gifts He's given you.  You may not always "feel" gifted, anointed or talented in your service to God.  There are times when you will have to fight apathy.  How do you get fired up? You stir yourself up! You fan the flame! You stoke the embers inside of you and you make yourself recognize, esteem and utilize the gifts God has given you! It's a choice. It's a discipline. It's vital! So, every now and then you just need to shake yourself, speak the Word, make a fresh commitment to use your gifts to serve God.

5.   1 Peter 4:10-11

Who has received a gift or gifts from God?_____

These gifts are also called the "manifold_____."

What are we to do with these gifts?_____

Who gives us the ability to use and flourish in the gifts?_____

## D. Your Place Will Be Exhalted As You Humble Yourself

Humility is the chief hallmark of any servant of God. In fact, God absolutely opposes the proud and pride causes downfalls. It is wise for all of us to consistently choose the road of humility over the road of pride. Humility is a choice. God does not humble us, because He already told us to humble ourselves. The Bible says that pride will cause us to be humbled, but God will not humble us. He will allow us to be humbled by pride and He will encourage us to humble ourselves!

Did you know that you don't always start out where you will end up in ministry? It's true in all of life. You must humble yourself, start at the beginning and trust God to exalt you in due time. Let's look at the power of humility.

1.   Isaiah 57:15

Who does God like to dwell with?_____

2.   Matthew 23:12

What happens to the person who exalts himself?_____

What happens to the person who humbles himself?_____

3.   James 4:6-10

What does God give the humble?_____

If we humble ourselves in God's sight, what does He do?_____

4.   1 Peter 5:5-6

Who does God resist?_____

Who gets grace?_____

When we humble ourselves, what does God do in due time?_____

# E. Your Place Will Increase As You Avoid These Pitfalls

1.  Avoid The Lone Ranger Syndrome

    Your piece in the puzzle is vital, and your piece needs to be connected to other pieces to be successful and to complete God's Box Top! One piece all by itself does not a puzzle make! The enemy likes to tap certain Christians on the shoulder and speak these lies into their ears:

    "C'mon, you don't need this church or these Christians. Besides, half of them are fake, phony, and definitely not as spiritual or committed as you. You're the most anointed one here. Look at how zealous you are! Why, everyone else is lukewarm. Just do your own thing—go preach the gospel all by yourself. You can do it alone."

    If you're not very mature or wise, you'll be flattered by these lies and you'll launch out and fall flat on your face! Lone rangers are not God's plan. We are the "Body of Christ"—not the "body part of Christ"—we need to be connected to the Body of Christ—the church, to be most effective. Ecclesiastes 4:9-12 makes this plain: "Two are better than one; because they have a good reward for their labour. For if they fall, the one will lift up his fellow: but woe to him that is alone when he falleth; for he hath not another to help him up. Again, if two lie together, then they have heat: but how can one be warm alone? And if one prevail against him, two shall withstand him; and a threefold cord is not quickly broken."

    Lone rangers are like the log that's been taken from the bonfire. If the log is placed several yards from the bonfire, it will continue to burn for a little while, but in time the fire will go out and the log will grow cold. The Bible tells us that two are better than one and God is not in favor of Lone Rangers.

2.  Avoid The Critic Syndrome

    Be on guard against this syndrome after you've had a great success. You may be tempted to judge others in the church. You may feel that they are not leading, doing church, youth ministry, worship, kids ministry or some other type of ministry the way you think it should be done. You may begin to feel superior and the enemy will work to puff your mind up with thoughts of your own greatness. Besides the fact that God hates pride and arrogance, a spirit of haughtiness will cost you opportunities.

    If you find yourself feeling jealous, envious or critical, beware! That's what happened to Saul. When he was little in his own sight, God gave him the opportunity to be the King over Israel, but after a few victories Saul got too big for his britches and did not obey the Lord. God called it rebellion and took the kingdom from Saul. Read the whole story in 1 Samuel 15:17-26.

3.    Avoid The Hyperspiritual Syndrome

It is a wonderful thing to be zealous for the Lord and to be sold out for His kingdom. However, be on guard against being "hyperspiritual" about every matter. Many things in life and in serving God are simply a matter of following common sense, using wisdom and putting one foot in front of the other! You should certainly inquire of the Lord and seek His wisdom on all facets of your life, but you don't need a sign, a dream, a vision or special angelic visit from God for confirmation on every decision. Let the Word of God be your standard and guide, use wisdom, walk in love and be a blessing—and you will avoid being hyperspiritual. Hyperspiritualism can be identified when you find yourself feeling the need to "use" spiritual phrases, excuses or explanations for your decisions and/or when you feel the need to impress someone with your spirituality.

For example, let's say your church has a need for nursery workers and you've been asked to help out in the nursery. Sometimes someone will say, "Well, I just don't feel led by the Lord to do that, Sister Sally. God has called me to deep intercession not diaper duty." Wrong answer! First, that doesn't sound like the heart of a servant—it sounds more like spiritual pride. Let's just use common sense. At your home, if the baby is crying and needs to be changed and you ask your oldest child to help you out with the baby, how would you feel if their response was, "Well mom, I just don't feel led by the Lord to help you with the baby. God has called me to go play basketball." It's bit ridiculous, isn't it? Yet, that is what many "hyperspiritual" Christians will do when asked to serve in an area of ministry they perceive as being beneath their spirituality. When was the last time you felt "led" to take out the trash? You use common sense and take the trash out because it needs to be done. If you're in a family you do what needs to be done, whether you feel "led" or not.

Don't overspiritualize serving God, just seek to be a blessing and assist where there is a need and God will be sure to promote you to "your ministry" in the right time.

# F. Application

God has a plan! He is looking for people who will hook up with His plan. Many times, as believers, we come up with our plans for how we can "help" God. Often, we ask God to bless our plans and our ideas without realizing that if we just hooked up with God's plans they are already blessed! A huge secret for living the fulfilled, fruitful, blessed Christian life is to simply understand God's plan and cooperate with Him and His ways of doing things. His plan is already blessed, so let's submit and yield to Him!

If you serve in the ministry of helps in your church in the areas of nursery, children's, youth, young adults, traffic team, welcome, ushers, praise and worship, men's, women's, and hospitality ministries or any other area of service, God wants to bless, teach, train, grow and promote you in your church! How? There are several basic Bible principles that will help you. Let's look at how to cooperate with God in your local church.

1.    Be Faithful With Your Time.

First, be faithful to attend church on a regular basis! The only way you can get to know the heartbeat of a church is to attend regularly. That doesn't mean you have to be there every time the doors are open, but determine to regularly attend Sunday mornings and/or Sunday night and/or the midweek service or programs as you are able. If you, by faith, choose to believe that God has called your pastor and leadership team and if you believe that God is giving them sermon material for your benefit, then you'll find the Holy Spirit will customize your pastor's messages just for you each time you attend!

If you are in the process of finding a church home, then visit a church for at least a month or more to get an accurate picture of what the church is all about. Make a point to get to know some of the people. Ask church leaders the questions that are important to you. Make the most of your time by attending a variety of things the church has to offer. We have observed that those people or families who are regular attenders of our church and doers of the Word that they hear are the most stable and blessed individuals and families as well. Be faithful with your time and attend your church on a regular basis.

2.  Be Faithful With Your Attitude.

Be teachable! Don't be a know-it-all. Be open to hear and receive God's Word. Avoid being critical. Do what the Bible says and walk in love—believing the best about everyone, including the pastor and the church leaders. Don't be easily offended if everyone doesn't reach out to you like you expect. You may need to take the initiative to meet people. You may need to investigate what types of programs, classes and activities the church has to offer. Be free from unrealistic expectations. Don't be a complainer or a whiner. Don't have an attitude that says, "Well, if I were running this church...I would do this...I wouldn't do that...I can't believe they are going to do this..." Church leaders are just ordinary people, called by God and doing their best to follow and obey His leading. Be merciful and supportive in your attitude. One negative spark can light a whole church on fire. If you can't say something nice or edifying to others in the church about the church, then don't say anything at all. If you find that you don't understand things that are happening in the church, then make it a point to talk directly to the pastor or those in leadership.

For example, sometimes unfortunate or illogical things happen in a church, and there are always at least two sides to every story! The goal of most pastors in difficult church situations is to walk in love and put the best light on the situation and individuals that they can. This means that although they know the whole story and could easily share "their slant" on situations, they generally try to share very little or only the "need to know" information with the congregation. In some cases, a pastor will actually take the "brunt end" of a situation so that others and their reputations won't be hurt. If you are not privy to all the information on every situation in your church, it is wise to keep a positive attitude and believe the best!

3.  Be Faithful With Your Talents.

The best way to feel a part of a church, to meet other people and to grow with a church family is to get involved! Use your talents and do something. Find out where and how you can get involved in the church. If there are classes to take, then sign up! Let the pastor, or those in leadership, know that you desire and are willing to get involved wherever they need help. You would be amazed at how significant your contribution to the church can be. Perhaps you are creative, technically-minded, musical, gifted to work with children, or maybe you have a bubbly, outgoing personality or great organizational skills. Be faithful to make your talents available. Don't be discouraged if you are aren't asked to do the very specific thing you wanted to do. Sometimes you need to prove yourself faithful in little things before you can be entrusted to do other things. Trust the pastor and the church leaders to use you where the needs are the greatest. In due season, as the Bible teaches, when God has counted you faithful, He will put you in the ministry that your heart desires.

4.    Be Faithful In Your Commitments.

Be a person of your word.  If you say that you will be somewhere, then be sure to follow through.  If you say that you will be involved in a particular part of the church, then be faithful to the end of your commitment.  Don't quit halfway through.  Did you know that there are always many "starters" but fewer "finishers"?  Anyone can start a class.  Anyone can start a ministry.  Anyone can start a race, but only those who are faithful in their commitments will finish!  Be faithful to prepare and fulfill your commitments.  Do everything with a spirit of excellence.  Avoid the "this is good enough to get by" mentality.  God's kingdom and the work of God deserve nothing less than excellence.  Pay attention to details and avoid being sloppy in your commitments.  Be the kind of person who can be counted upon.  Be the kind of person that exemplifies commitment.

5.    Be Faithful With Your Resources.

Be faithful to use your resources—your time, your finances, your material goods–to bless others and to further the Gospel through your church.  If God has enabled you to prosper in financial and material things, be generous in your giving. Remember, God has given you the ability to obtain wealth so that He may establish His covenant in the earth. (Deuteronomy 8:18)  He certainly wants you as a believer to be blessed in life and to enjoy abundance, but be sure to keep a healthy perspective on cheerful and generous giving.  The Bible teaches that the tithe, which is ten percent of your increase or income, belongs to the Lord and should be brought to the storehouse—the local church that you attend.  In addition, we are commanded by God to give offerings to worthy ministries that are propagating the gospel of the Lord Jesus Christ and to give alms to those who are poor and in need of material things.

It is sad to say that many Christians will trust God in other areas of their lives, but when it comes to money, they keep a tight grip on their wallets.  Don't have a stingy spirit.  Be known as a giver.  Be known as a generous person.  Be faithful with your material and financial resources by giving to your local church first and to others as God leads you. Be a faithful channel God can flow through in the area of giving.  Trust God to multiply your giving back to you, so that you will have more to live from and more to give.

[1] Biblesoft's New Exhaustive Strong's Numbers and Concordance with Expanded Greek-Hebrew Dictionary. Copyright (c) 1994, Biblesoft and International Bible Translators, Inc.

[2] Ibid.

# HOW TO FUNCTION IN YOUR LOCAL CHURCH

God has set up His Headquarters in nearly every city! His HQ is the local church! The local church is God's outpost. Local churches are God's harvesting machines for a community. Local churches are God's hospital for His people. Local churches are His boot camps for His soldiers. Jesus loves and is building the local church, and it's vital that we understand how to function in our local church.

Of course, each local church is going to have its own culture and personality. Some churches have a congregationally-led style of government, while others are pastor-led, or elder board led. No two local churches are alike. Much of the personality of a local church will be a direct reflection of the calling, gifts, passions, anointing and graces on the senior leadership. One local church may emphasize ministry to families, while another local church is known for its music ministry. One local church may focus on reaching the poor and homeless, while another local church may focus on providing a Christian school to the community. One local church may be strong in Bible teaching, while another local church is strong in evangelism. One church may be traditional, while another church is contemporary. One local church may use the church organ to sing hymns and prefer a more stoic worship style, while another church may employ a ten-piece band and prefer a more upbeat worship style.

We see a great description of this in Ephesians 4:16: "From him the whole body, joined and held together by every supporting ligament, grows and builds itself up in love, as each part does its work." (NIV) In other words, the whole global universal church is joined together and growing according to the support and supply each local church supplies to the whole! As each local church does its work, the whole Body is benefited!

While there will be some differences in the exact approach from church to church, let's look at some basic things regarding how we function in the local church.

## A. Local Church 101 - God Wants Us To Know How To Behave

1. 1 Timothy 3:15

   What did the Apostle Paul want us to know?_____

2. 1 Corinthians 14:33,40

   What does God not author?_____

   How does God want things to operate?_____

   It's important that we understand how to behave in the church. God is not running a chaotic, casual, disorganized, do-your-own thing, disrespectful, mismanaged operation! Let's look at this subject more closely.

# B. Local Church 101 - God Wants Us To Understand His Flow Chart

Let's take a few moments to understand the basics of how God is managing His Body.  Aren't you glad that the God-head—God the Father, Jesus the Head of the Church and the Holy Spirit—is the best CEO on planet Earth?  God knows how to run a tight ship.  He knows how to manage His people properly and with precision.  He knows how to maximize His human resources.  He uses His people wisely, based upon His callings and giftings, by growth and experience, and by things that have been foreordained. God is the best manager in the universe.  He is organized, detailed and excellent with His human resources.  Let's look at how He has outlined His flow chart in the Word.

1.   Three Categories of Spiritual Gifts

The Bible describes various spiritual gifts that God gives to His children. These are supernatural gifts, graces and/or offices given by God to every believer when they are born-again. These are spiritual gifts, not natural gifts.

When it comes to natural gifts—these are important, too. Our natural gifts are God-given, but they are different than our spiritual gifts. Both our natural gifts and our spiritual gifts work together to help us fulfill God's plan for our lives.

You can identify your natural gifts by utilizing some of the popular temperament tests and personality profiles. In addition, the study of birth order and love languages can add another dimension to one's personality make-up and particular strengths and weaknesses.  I highly recommend that you consider any of these profile tests to gain a better working knowledge of how God has wired you for His kingdom.  (For a list of resources, please see the Appendix.)

When it comes to our spiritual gifts, the Bible describes three main categories of gifts. Many times in studying the Bible on this subject people will lump all the spiritual gifts mentioned in the Bible into one big pile, but it is helpful to break them out categorically. For our study we are going to classify them into these three main categories:

Motivational Gifts
Gifts of the Spirit
Ministry Office Gifts

We are going to take a bird's eye view look at and dissect these three general categories of spiritual gifts listed in the Bible.

2.   Motivational Gifts

The first category of spiritual gifts we will look at are called: motivational gifts.

One or more of the motivational gifts are given to EVERY believe when they are born again.

When you become a born-again Christian you are given a spiritual gift(s), which we are calling a "motivational gift". In other words, you have been gifted with a God-given "motivation" for doing certain things.  God endows you with His ability to do something that will benefit His kingdom and help your "piece" fulfill your purpose.  Every single believer has been given one or more motive gifts, and it is wise to be a good steward of those gifts and employ them in serving

God and His kingdom. For example, one believer may love to serve behind the scenes and be a helper, while another believer has a love for teaching children.  These are evidence of God's motive gifts.  Perhaps you know a Christian who is exceptional in their giving, while another displays an amazing amount of mercy.  Again, this is in part due to the motivational gifts that God has given them.

Let's look at these motivational gifts:

a.    Romans 12:4-8

What has God given every member of the Body of Christ according to verses 5 and 6?

_____

List the seven gifts mentioned:

_____            _____

_____            _____

_____            _____

_____

God "graces" us with one or more of these motivational gifts and then we are to operate in this gift by faith.

b.    1 Peter 4:10-11

According to this passage, who has received a gift?_____

What is the gift called in verse 10?_____

What does God expect us to do with the gift?_____

Notice verse 11 describes two categories—"speaking" gifts and "serving" gifts.  Some people are gifted and motivated to speak, write or create things to articulate the heart of God, while others are gifted and motivated to serve in a non-speaking capacity.

What attitude are those who "speak" and those who "serve/minister" supposed to have?

_____

The ultimate purpose of all the motivational gifts is to do what?

_____

3.   Gifts of The Spirit

The second category of spiritual gifts we will look at are called: gifts of the Spirit.

These particular gifts of the Spirit are given to ANY believer as the Holy Spirit desires.

These supernatural gifts of the Spirit are given as the Spirit wills to any believer that needs them at a particular time or for God's particular purposes.  The purpose of the gifts of the Spirit is that everyone may profit from it.  These gifts are not to be manufactured by human desire, but they are manifested as believers yield to the Spirit.  The key for operating in the gifts of the Spirit is yieldedness.  These gifts are given at the Spirit's discretion.  Many times, as a person recognizes that God has used him or her in a particular gift of the Spirit, they may find it easier to yield to the Spirit and be used by God in that particular gift.

Let's look at the gifts of the Spirit:

a.   1 Corinthians 12:1-11

What does God want according to verse 1?_____

In verse 7, the manifestation of the gifts of the Spirit is given for what reason?

_____

List the nine gifts of the Spirit mentioned in verses 8-10.

_____        _____

_____        _____

_____        _____

_____        _____

_____

The gifts of the Spirit are supernatural gifts given to individuals as needed for the profit of others, and as the Spirit wills.  We cannot manufacture or dictate when these gifts will be given.  We can simply give the Holy Spirit a place in our lives and yield to Him when He chooses to distribute these gifts to us.  These spiritual gifts can be grouped into three subcategories:

•   Revelation Gifts of the Spirit – those that reveal something of God's knowledge or insight, that is:  the word of wisdom, the word of knowledge, the discerning of spirits.

- Power Gifts of the Spirit – those that display God's supernatural power, that is: the gift of faith, the working of miracles, the gifts of healings.

- Utterance Gifts of the Spirit – those that say something, that is: the gift of prophecy, the gifts of speaking in tongues, the gift of interpretation of tongues.

Are these gifts given to everyone or only to some individuals?_____

According to verse 11, who determines the distribution of the gifts of the Spirit?

_____

The gifts of the Spirit are not given to everyone, but they are given to whoever needs them at a particular time as the Spirit determines.

4.  Ministry Office Gifts

The last category of spiritual gifts we will look at are called: ministry office gifts.

These gifts are given to SOME believers according to the Lord's calling.

The Bible describes what is known as the five-fold ministry office gifts in Ephesians 4. The ministry office gifts are: Apostle, Prophet, Evangelist, Pastor, and Teacher.

These ministry offices are directly related to God's calling. God calls some people, not all people, to stand in these offices vocationally and take a servant-leadership role in His kingdom. God calls, anoints and appoints.

a.  Ephesians 4:11-16

Are these gifts that everyone receives or just some? _____

(Notice if you back up to verse 7 that "each one" has received spiritual gifts, but in verse 11, only "some" have received a call to the ministry offices listed.)

What type of ministry office gifts did God give?

_____    _____    _____

_____    _____

What is the purpose of these ministry office gifts?

_____

This passage is a classic one describing leadership offices in the Body of Christ and their responsibility to train and equip members in the Body of Christ for service. God has called "some" people to these ministry gift offices, but not everyone. These five offices represent the five leading roles on God's executive team of oversight in the Body of Christ.

b.   1 Corinthians 12:27-28

Has God set all people or some people in the church to stand in these ministry offices?

_____

List the offices "in the church" as listed in verse 28.

_____

_____

What does the progression and overlap of the motivational gifts, the gifts of the Spirit and the ministry office gifts look like? Let's look at a common progression. Let's say God has called and gifted someone to ultimately stand in a full-time ministry office of: apostle, prophet, evangelist, pastor or teacher. Before they function in that office, there will likely be a lengthy season of faithfulness before they are appointed to function in the ministry office gift God has called them to. They will usually experience years of growth that include: personal encounters with God, growth in the Word, ministry training, experience in serving, and perhaps an assistant's position or apprenticeship. It is rare that God would jumpstart or fast track someone into a ministry gift office; they would need to be qualified and equipped by developing history with God. God does not appoint a novice into these positions, but as a person is called, proves themselves faithful and is a good steward over the motivational gifts and the gifts of the Spirit God has given them, then God may appoint an individual to a ministry office. These ministry office gifts are not a self-appointed positions, but a God-called offices.

Let's look at the other ministry office gifts. Some are called to serve in the ministry office of Evangelist—and they preach the gospel to the lost and they stir up and equip the Body of Christ to do the work of evangelism! Some are called to serve in the ministry office of Teacher, to the Body of Christ—and they provide rich line-upon-line Bible teaching to build up the Body. Some are called to serve in the ministry office of Apostle or Prophet—and they serve as a voice to pioneer and lay foundations in the the Body of Christ by the Word, by the Spirit and through missionary endeavors at home and abroad. Some are called to serve in the ministry office of Pastor—and they serve to oversee, lead and feed the local flock of God. The Bible gives us definitions and qualifications for each of these ministry offices.

It's possible that a person may stand in one or more ministry offices. For example, we see that with several of the disciples and the Apostle Paul. It would not be uncommon for a person to stand in the ministry office of a Pastor/Teacher—as one who was gifted to feed and lead the flock, as well as provide rich line-upon-line Bible teaching. Another person may be called to the ministry office combination of Pastor/Evangelist and be gifted to feed and lead the flock while stirring up believers to reach the lost. Someone may be called to the ministry office combination of Apostle/Teacher and may serve as a pioneer on the mission field—establishing a gospel work among unreached people and teaching them the Word of God in line-upon-line fashion. There are any number of ministry office gift combinations possible—as the Lord deems necessary.

God's diversity in dispensing the spiritual gifts is exciting!

5.  Let's Summarize The Three Categories of Spiritual Gifts

    a.  Motivational Gifts: God has given EACH member of the Body of Christ one or more motive gifts. The motivational gifts can be categorized as either serving gifts or speaking gifts. It's our responsibility as good stewards to identify, and by faith use the gifts God has given us to benefit the Body. (Romans 12:4-8 and 1 Peter 4:10)

    b.  Gifts of the Spirit: The Holy Spirit gives ANY member of the Body of Christ any of the gifts of the Spirit, as mentioned in 1 Corinthians 12, as He wills and as is needed for the profiting of all. God outlines the order in which these gifts should be used, and gives us guidelines for the public ministry of the gifts of the Spirit. These are supernatural gifts, given by the Holy Spirit as needed, and it is our responsibility to covet these gifts and to stay yielded to the Spirit and available to Him if He should choose to use us in any of these particular gifts of the Spirit. (1 Corinthians 12; 13:1; 14)

    c.  Ministry Office Gifts: God calls and gifts SOME members of the Body of Christ to function and serve in a ministry office. This would be more of a full-time or vocational calling to serve in what is commonly known as the five-fold ministry as listed in Ephesians 4. These ministerial management offices are God-called, not man- or self-appointed. God gifts people and calls some to stand in these offices for the purpose of equipping and building up the Body of Christ as a whole to do the work of the ministry. (Ephesians 4:11-16 and 1 Corinthians 12:28)

6.  Let's Look At A Few Questions and Scenarios

    a.  Teachers: Do I have the *motivational gift of teaching* or am I called to the *ministry office of a teacher*?

        Let's say a person in the church has been given a gift to teach. How do they know if this is the motivational gift of teaching as listed in Romans 12 or the ministry office of teacher as listed in Ephesians 4? How does a person discern their gift to teach properly? First, it is necessary to rightly divide God's Word and understand that there are at least two types of teachers listed in the Bible.

        The first type of teacher are those with the motivational gift of teaching and they would teach in the "ministry of helps" within their local church. For example, there are many people whom God has gifted to teach—perhaps in children's ministry, adult classes, youth ministry, women's ministry, small groups or other areas. This motivational gift of teaching is a tremendous help to the local church!

        The second category of teacher would be those to whom God has given a motivational gift of teaching as well as the calling and gifts needed to stand in the ministry office of teacher. This person is called to teach the Body of Christ at large. Many of the local, regional and national ministers you and I know would be in this category—their influence as a teacher extends beyond the reaches of their local church to the Body of Christ at large. They may teach at conferences, by traveling to various churches or through mass communication. They may teach through their writings, books, media or online ministry. By standing in the ministry office of teacher and employing their gifts, they would be used by God to equip and build up the Body of Christ.

The interesting note is that most, if not all, of those who have been successful in their calling to the ministry office of the teacher began by using their motive gift to teach in the ministry of helps in their local church. When God counted them faithful in their service under another man's ministry, He saw fit to promote them and place them in the ministry office of teacher He had called them to fill. Can you see this?

b.  Pastors: What about the varieties of pastors and their different callings and styles? Let's say God calls three different people to the office of pastor, and each one of those pastors has a different flair. Why is this? This is a manifestation of the various natural temperaments added to the various spiritual gifts God has given to each individual. For example, there may be one pastor with an outgoing temperament who seems to have the motivational gift of mercy and teaching; while another pastor with a risk-taking temperament and the motivational gift of leadership is more inclined toward winning the lost. Both of these people stand in the office of the pastor, but they operarte with different natural temperaments and different motivational gifts. This is evidence of people called to the same ministry office, but operating with different motivational gifts. This is an example of the "manifold grace of God!" Isn't it wonderful?

It might be helpful to know that in a local church, the Pastor is the primary God-appointed leader. The Pastor may have a staff, board of elders or deacons, advisors, or others who assist in the oversight of the church, but the Pastor is the primary leader and it is through the ministry office of the Pastor that God will lead the local church. While God has not called Pastors to run a "dictatorial regime", the Pastor is the one who will be held most accountable for the feeding and the leading of the sheep and the Pastor will be held accountable for carrying out the vision God has given him/her for that particular local church. Wise Pastors surround themselves with godly counselors, elders, deacons, boards, accountability partners and committee members. While these roles are appreciated, it is helpful if all those who serve in leadership in a church understand and esteem the fact that God Himself has called, anointed and appointed the Pastor with the particular grace/spiritual gifts needed and placed him/her in the ministry office of Pastor.

Unfortunately church wars have been fought over who is going to have "control" of the church. Will it be the worship leader? The member with the most seniority? The deacon board? The wealthiest member? How much power should the Pastor have? Isn't it the elders role to keep the Pastor's feet to the fire? We can see from Scripture that the Pastor will be the one with the primary responsibility before God for the leadership and stewardship of the church.

c.  Don't get crazy! Sometimes when it comes to any of the gifts we've studied, people don't use common sense! We've had baby Christians tell us that they know God has called them to be a prophet and they want to begin "prophesying" all kinds of things to us. God is not going to violate His own laws of good management! He doesn't authorize a novice to jump into a senior management position overnight! He trains and grooms and develops a novice through a season of growth, service in the ministry of helps and character development. If someone is gifted or called to function in any of the motive gifts, gifts of the Spirit or ministry office gifts, they will first have a long season of proving themselves faithful. When God counts them faithful, He will put them in the ministry He has ordained one phase at a time. The bottom line is to be faithful in using the gifts God has given you to be a blessing to others.

God is not a cookie cutter Manager! He gives good grace/spiritual gifts to the right people at the right time for the right reasons and seasons. He is so creative and innovative and employs so many types of administrations, operations and manifestations to build His church! It is a great joy to serve a God who is so generous and innovative in His gift giving!

On the other hand, He has prescribed the way, the heart and the character that is required for maximizing all of His grace/spiritual gifts and these various areas of service in His Body. It's our duty to be good stewards over every gift.

Do you have a better idea of how to function in your local church? God has a place reserved just for you! One key ingredient to functioning, flowing and being fruitful in any of the gifts God gives us is a working knowledge of God's plan for spiritual authority. In the next chapter, let's talk about how to flourish and flow with the spiritual authority God has developed.

# C. Application

What do you do if you do feel God calling you to some type of ministry office, in a full-time vocational way? Perhaps you are called by God to serve as a Pastor or Evangelist or Teacher or in some other capacity. What steps should you take?

It is important that you use wisdom as you pursue the calling and direction you feel God has placed in your heart. It's important that you pray and spend time in God's Word to let Him speak and confirm His call to your heart. It is very wise to seek good counsel from godly people who know you. Being called by God, sensing the zeal of God, and feeling His Word like a fire shut up in your bones is a wonderful and divine thing, but it also requires acting with wisdom so that all that God intends can come to full fruition in your life. Being willing to "leave all" for the gospel is a noble thing.

Unfortunately, some young Christians in their zeal and lack of knowledge of God's Word have foolishly "left all" for the Gospel. Some have quit their jobs, left their families, not paid their bills, gone into the streets and preached hellfire and brimstone, while running from their responsibilities as a citizen, as a husband or wife, as a parent and as an employee. Oftentimes, these types of people become a menace and burden to society, and their bad reputations affect the Body of Christ in a negative way. When they "left all", they left their common sense as well. This is not God's plan and this type of irresponsible lifestyle does not glorify God or further the cause of Christ.

The important thing, as a sincere Christian, is to have a heart attitude that says, "Lord, I will give You my life. I will do what You want me to do. I will go where You want me to go. I will say what You want me to say." It may be that the Lord will have you do just exactly what you are already doing, except now you will be doing it to glorify Him.

On the other hand, God does call some people to leave their current vocation and status in life in order to serve Him in a full-time vocation. Often times this type of call will include some type of formal ministerial training or an apprenticeship under a seasoned minister of the Gospel. God is not in the business of raising up "flash in the pan" superstar ministers. The types of people God uses are likely to experience years of developing a history with God. Over time, when God counts an individual faithful, He will put them in the ministry.

If you sense the call of God on your life, it is wise to speak with your pastor, or an older, mature Christian who knows you. God's timing and His wisdom are important ingredients when it comes to these matters.

# HOW TO FOLLOW GOD'S PLAN FOR SPIRITUAL AUTHORITY

One of the most liberating truths you will ever learn is this subject of spiritual authority. Unfortunately, because of unbalanced teaching, this subject has created great confusion, and been misrepresented. "Control freak" pastors and church leaders have majored on "submission" while abusing overly submissive church members; and rebellious "maverick" church members have minored on "submission" while being responsible for strife and numerous church splits. God does not authorize either excess. Let's gain the Biblical understanding of God's plan for submission and authority that will truly set you free!

In this chapter we will be focusing on spiritual authority as it relates to God's Church and His government and management style. Spiritual authority begins with God the Father, through Jesus His Son and by the great Holy Spirit. God is not confused. He is not disorganized or running His Church by the "seat of the pants" management style. He is very precise and structured, and yet provides for an atmosphere of great liberty and freedom. His "infrastructure" is the highest and the best! Let's look at it.

## A. Jesus Is The Head Of The Church - He Calls The Shots

What does the Bible call Jesus?

1. Colossians 1:18 _____

2. Colossians 2:19 _____

3. Ephesians 1:20-23 _____

4. John 10:10-20 _____

5. Hebrews 13:20 _____

Jesus is the Head of the Church! He is the Shepherd of the sheep. He has all authority. All authority has been given to Him and He delegates spiritual authority to those whom He has called and those who have met the qualifications outlined in His Word. We all agree that Jesus is the Head of the Church, but to whom has Jesus delegated authority over His local churches? Let's look at who carries spiritual authority in God's Church.

## B. Jesus Gives Authority In His Church To His Ministers

1. Ephesians 4:11-16

a.   What gifts and calling did Jesus give to some?  List the five-fold ministry offices described in Ephesians.

_____

b.   What is the purpose and responsibility of those to whom Jesus has delegated spiritual authority in His church?

_____

c.   What is the Body supposed to look like as God's delegates do their job?

_____

Jesus is the Head of the church and the Great Shepherd of the sheep.  He is the most excellent Manager and Overseer in the universe!  He has delegated spiritual authority and oversight responsibilities to some members of His Body.  As we discussed in the previous chapter, the five-fold ministers have specific roles within the Body of Christ at large.  These ministers (or in modern terms we may call them "middle managers"), will be held account-able for the job they do.  It's important that they understand their role and that those of us under their authority understand our place as well.  The key leader in any given local church is the Senior Pastor.  This is the person, along with those to whom they have delegated spiritual authority, who will be held primarily responsible for the leading and feeding of the flock.  Let's look at the role of the Pastor in local churches.

2.   1 Peter 5:2-4

What are Pastors (Jesus' undershepherds) supposed to do?

_____

Pastors are called by Jesus to "feed" and "lead" the flock of God.  They are to have the oversight of a local church and they are to lead, not by force or domination, but by love and by being an example.  This is a high calling of servant-hood.

3.   Jeremiah 3:15

God gives us a great picture of His view of the Pastor's role.  Describe the Pastors God delegates authority to.

_____

A lack of understanding about the role of a Pastor has created much heartbreak and caused multiplied offenses. People who were not called to the office of Pastor, and therefore not authorized or responsible before God for the oversight of the church, have tried to push, control or manipulate their agendas, opinions and views on a particular church and have been guilty of creating confusion, church splits and discord among the church.  Church board mem-bers with wrong motives, wealthy business people looking for control in the church, power hungry church members and busybodies have done more to damage the church and undermine the role of a Pastor than just about any other force.  It is simply a lack of understanding regarding this area of spiritual authority.

Every church member is absolutely entitled to have an opinion about their church, but they would be wise to keep that opinion to themselves unless it is asked for.  Some people think they have a "right" to voice their opinions and even cloak it as a "prayer concern", while other people think they have a right to give their two-cent's worth, but if the truth were known, many of those opinions and "two cents" do nothing more than undermine God's plan for a local church and/or discredit the Pastor's leadership in the church.  God does not wink at it; He takes it quite seriously.  Let's look at the seriousness of this subject further.

## C. Jesus Gives Authority "Over" To Those Who Submit "Under"

1.  Matthew 8:5-10 and Luke 7:1-10

In this great story, Jesus gives us insight into the operation of authority.

a.  In Matthew 8:9, the centurion described his authority.  What did he say?

_____

b.  In Matthew 8:10, what was Jesus' response to the centurion?

_____

We learn a simple principle in this passage.  We cannot have authority "over" until we are submitted "under" authority.  The centurion recognized that Jesus was "under" the authority of His Father and therefore His words had authority "over" all sickness and disease.  Jesus saw that this centurion was a man "under" authority and therefore he had been given authority "over" one hundred other men who obeyed his words.

The first major principle for having spiritual authority "over" is that you must be "under" spiritual authority.  What type of spiritual authority do we need to be "under"?

## D. Jesus Looks For Those Who Submit To God And His Word

1.  Submit To God

James 4:6-10

In verse 7, what are we told to do?_____

Does God force us to "submit" to Him?_____

Who does God resist?_____

2.  Submit To God's Word

a.   Psalm 138:2

What has God exalted even above His Name?_____

b.   Psalm 119:105

What is supposed to direct our steps?_____

We are to submit first and foremost to God Himself and then to His Word.  God and His Word are to be the standard by which we measure our lives.  They are to have the highest place in our heart, decision making, and day-to-day living.

## E. Jesus Looks For Those Who Submit To His Delegates

Unfortunately, this is what "separates the men from the boys!"  Everyone can say they are submitted to God and to His Word, but where the rubber really meets the road is where submitting to God's delegates is concerned. This is where the difficulties begin!  Let's look at this subject and talk about avoiding some of the ditches that have created heartbreak in many churches.

1.   You Cannot Say You Submit To God And Not Submit To His Delegates

a.   1 John 4:20

What does this verse tell us about loving God whom we cannot see and hating our brother whom we can see?

_____

In other words, it's easy to say, "I love the Lord", whom we've never seen and in the same breath say, "I just don't love my brother", whom we can see.  God says this person is liar – he really doesn't love God at all!  In the same way, a person can say, "I submit to God", whom he's never seen and in the same breath say, "I just don't submit to men", whom he can see.  God would say this person is a liar, too – he really doesn't submit to God at all.  If he cannot submit to the ones God has delegated His authority to, he is not submitted to God either.

b.   Hebrews 13:7,17

In verse 7, what are we told to do?_____

Notice, as followers we are advised to check out the way of life and the fruit of the life of those we follow.  We are not asked to follow an ungodly leader.  We have a responsibility to follow those whose way of life and outcome in life are representative of the Lord.  We are to follow those who follow Christ.
(1 Corinthians 11:1)

In verse 17, what are we told to do?_____

What will be required of those who have spiritual authority?

_____

In what way are we to submit to those who have spiritual authority?

_____

If we submit in a way that brings joy to our spiritual authorities, what benefit do we get?

_____

If we submit in a way that is troublesome, what is the result?

_____

The way you submit is as important as the fact that you submit. This is clearly seen in children. If you are a parent, you've seen your children submit to your authority with a cheerful attitude and the result is that they are blessed and you are pleased. On the other hand, you've had moments when your child submitted to your authority with a bad attitude, roll of an eye and a mouth that was mumbling some complaint. The result is that you were frustrated and that child did not win any favor by their attitude. It wasn't a joy and it was unprofitable for them. This is what Hebrews is describing.

c. 1 Thessalonians 5:12-13, 1 Peter 5:1-5

Describe the relationship between Pastors/church leaders and church members. What is the Pastor/church leaders role?

_____

How should you view your Pastor and other spiritual authorities in your life?

_____

2. Avoid The Aaron, Miriam, Korah, Dathan And Abiram Syndrome

These are classic cases of rebelling against God's delegated authorities. This is not smart. If you want to get on God's bad side in a hurry, begin to murmur, complain and rebel against His delegates. Let's look at what happened to Aaron, Miriam and Korah, Dathan and Abiram.

a.    Numbers 12:1-13

In verse 1, what was Miriam and Aaron's first mistake?

_____

In verse 2, describe their attitude and words.

_____

Who heard their words?_____

In other words, Miriam and Aaron began to get critical. A critical spirit is the first step down the slippery slope of rebellion. Always be on guard against being critical. Because they were critical of the leader God had chosen and appointed, they opened their mouths and voiced their criticism. The second step of rebellion is evidenced by a person's mouth. Always put a guard on your lips. Their words really described the problem. They didn't like the choices Moses was making. They didn't like his leadership! Notice the tone of their words in verse 2. In essence, they were saying, "Who made you the big cheese? Why do you have to lead everything? You're not the only one God speaks to. We can hear from God, too. Why are we following you? Maybe you should listen to us. After all, you already made a bad decision by marrying that girl from Egypt..." God heard it all! And God was not amused.

In verse 3, how is Moses described?_____

Do you see or hear "meekness" in Aaron or Miriam?_____

In verse 4-9, how did God respond to Aaron and Miriam?

_____

_____

God made it clear to Aaron and Miriam that He Himself had chosen Moses as His representative and God presented Moses' credentials to them in straightforward fashion.

In verse 8, how did God describe their words?_____

In verse 8, how did God describe Moses?_____

In verse 9, what was God's response to Aaron and Miriam?

_____

In verse 10, what was the result of their sin?_____

In verse 11, Aaron recognized their error and did the right thing.  What did he do?

_____

In verse 13, we get a glimpse of the heart of Moses, the leader God had chosen.  What did Moses do?

_____

b.   Numbers 16:1-50

Korah was a leader Moses had appointed.  In verses 2-3, we see that he had a change of heart toward Moses and his leadership.  What did Korah do?

_____

Paraphrase, in your own words, the complaint/criticism of Korah.

_____

Do you see the picture?  Korah was one of the leaders in Israel.  God had called Korah to a leadership position; he was "over" the service of the tabernacle and yet he was "under" Moses' leadership.  One day, Korah decided to overstep his God-given authority and position.  Korah gathered many of Moses' influential followers to join him in murmuring against Moses and Aaron.  The essence of his words was much like those of Aaron and Miriam in Numbers 12: "Hey Moses, you are in control of too much.  You are doing too much.  We all know God, not just you.  God is among us and we can hear from Him just fine.  Who put you in charge?  You're just a self-appointed leader and we've about had it with you..." Notice Moses' response.  He responded by humility and truth.  Moses said in essence, "Let God answer your complaint.  Let's see whom God has chosen to be the leader."

In verse 11, God took Korah's complaints personally.  Who were Korah's criticisms described as being against?

_____

In verse 12, we see that Korah's rebellious attitude had infected other leaders.  Who are they?

_____

Describe their rebellious attitude in verses 12-14.

_____

Moses called for a meeting with these leaders. When they presented themselves before Moses, what had they done to the heart of the congregation according to verse 19?

_____

In verses 21, 24, and 26, what did the Lord tell Moses, Aaron and the congregation to do?

_____

Verses 30-35 describe the judgment of God on the rebellion of Korah, Dathan and Abiram. What happened?

_____

_____

In verse 42, the rebellious attitude of Korah, Dathan and Abiram had permeated the congregation and they murmured against Moses and Aaron. God would not put up with it and His judgment on their critical spirit opened the door for a plague to begin in Israel. Describe Moses' response.

_____

_____

In the end, how many people were destroyed because of the critical, rebellious spirit of Korah?

_____

_____

Can you see the devastation that occurs when people do not submit to God's delegated authorities? Can you see how the Lord feels about rebellion? Can you see how infectious a critical spirit can be? As helpers and leaders in a local church, it's vital that we guard our hearts and mouths. Poor attitudes, a critical spirit and a loose mouth can be the downfall of any believer and/or church leader, so let's be wise and honor the Lord by how we honor those God has joined us to.

Do you see the importance and value of flowing with the spiritual authority structure God has ordained? Can you see the liberty it provides? Can you see the safety it brings? Can you see that it clarifies who will be responsible and accountable for what? Those who will be held responsible also carry the authority that goes with that responsibility.

Let's conclude this chapter by looking at the following example. I once heard a minister share this illustration of authority by describing the difference between being in the army of God versus being in the family of God.

Imagine a military family of three men – one father and two sons. The father serves in the Army as a General. The oldest son serves as a Colonel and the younger son serves as a Sargeant. During battle, it's vital that this family understands submission and authority! If the General gives an order, it's imperative that his sons respond with a "Yes, sir"; not with a "Yea, but Dad..." response! Operating according to rank is an important part of a successful army. However, when it's Christmas and the family is home for the holidays and at the Christmas dinner meal, the "rank" is not in effect any longer. The youngest son can have as many mashed potatoes as his father. The oldest son can eat just as much pumpkin pie as his father and younger brother. At the dinner table, they are family and there is no rank! On the battlefield, they are soldiers and submitting to rank is vital for their success.

In the same way, as Christians we are in both the "family of God" and the "army of God". It's important that when we are doing kingdom business and operating in the "battle" for winning souls and building up the Body through our local churches, we submit to those who have spiritual authority over us. God has chosen to call, anoint and appoint certain people to carry specific rank and in this environment we need to have the "Yes, sir" mentality! However, at other times in day-to-day living, we pull up to God's banquet table and our cup runs over! There are enough blessings for everyone in God's family to enjoy! This illustration paints a great picture for understanding the principle of spiritual authority.

# F. Application

What do you do when you are frustrated in a church? What if your heart is no longer engaged with the church and it's vision? How do you deal with your opinion or discontent when you view your pastor or other church leaders as imperfect or ungodly?

1. First, You Need To Remember There Is No Such Thing As A Perfect Church!

   You will be chasing an enigma if you are searching for the perfect church! Likewise, there are no perfect people living on planet Earth - not even church leaders or your pastor! You'll have to make a decision to extend mercy and grace to any church and church leaders you are involved with!

2. Second, You Need To Separate And Discern Your Frustration.

   Can you determine if your frustration is related to something that offended you? Is your frustration due to a change of grace, a new season or a change of heart on your part? Is your frustration due to something as simple as your own difficulty with a personality quirk in your pastor or other church leader?

   If you've been offended and have not dealt with it, you will carry that offense to every church and into every relationship you pursue. Offenses are like bitter roots that take hold in our hearts if they are not uprooted. If your heart and season of life is changing, then perhaps the grace you have had in your church is shifting and you'll need to spend some time in prayer to discern where God's grace is directing you. If your frustration is due to a personality conflict, you need to realize that we all have different personalities and ideosynchrasies, and sometimes they clash. Is your frustration due to the fact that you simply don't enjoy the personality style of your pastor or leader? If so, perhaps you need to spend more time praying FOR your pastor. You may find that God will change your own heart, and the very thing that used to bug you now endears you to your pastor!

3. Third, You Need To Ask Honest Questions.

   Do you believe God has called you to attend and be actively involved in this church? Do you believe in the vision of this church? Do you believe in the leadership of this church? Do you believe your pastor has a heart for God? Do you believe their heart and motives are in the right place? Do you believe they are doing the best they can?

   If you believe that at the core God has called you to participate in this church and you agree with and can support the vision of the church, and if you believe that the Pastor and the leadership of the church are good people who love

God and are doing their best to follow Him, then again you need to pray! You need to pray FOR your church, FOR the vision of your church and FOR your pastor and church leadership team! You will be amazed at the grace that will be given to him or her simply because you prayed.

If you believe that God is changing the season of your church involvement, or if you cannot support the vision of your church, or if you believe that your Pastor or church leadership are living in an ungodly way or have the wrong motives, then you need to seriously pray about finding another church home. Generally speaking, it is not your job to change the direction, vision or structure of your church. It is not your role to change your pastor or to "correct" him or her. If you reach a place of utter internal frustration in your church experience, you would be wise to pray about finding another church home where you can commit to the church and its God-given vision with your heart and where you can respect and honor your pastor.

4.    Fourth, You Need To Make A Decision.

You need to decide to either stay involved with your church with your whole heart or leave your church gracefully. If you choose to stay involved in your church, be determined to engage your whole heart! If you need to forgive others, or ask others for forgiveness or initiate honest communication with others, then do so! Get your heart clear and then choose to walk in love and be a big blessing to your church, your church leaders and your pastor.

If you choose to leave your church, do it gracefully! Here's what you should NOT do! Don't spew negative, bitter gossip. Keep a guard on your mouth. You will be sowing seeds to your own future by how you handle your transition from one church to another. You should choose to speak good things, put the church and the leaders in the best possible light and focus on the positive experiences and blessings you have received during your time at that church. Do not gather a group of "rebels" around you! There will always be a group of people who will rally to the disheartened and it would be wise to NOT foster a group of complainers and murmurers and grumblers. Just remember Korah! To leave a church, just keep a sweet spirit and trust God with your future! If you operate in this way you will be blessed! In the event God is leading you to another church, be sure of this: He will always lead you out with joy and you'll be led forth with peace. So, if you are planning to leave a church with a grudge, bitterness or an offended spirit, you need to spend some serious time in prayer and perhaps honest communication with your church leader. Allow God to do a work in your own heart, so that you can leave with a good attitude, joy and peace!

Here's a final note, if you have left a church in the past and you left with a chip on your shoulder, blaming others, rationalizing why "they" were all wrong and "you" were all right, and if there was a rift in your departure, you may need to do some real soul searching and be sure your heart is right before God. You may need to make a phone call, write a letter or apologize for your fault in the way you handled things and the things you said. You may need to forgive those who mistreated you. The bottom line is that you want your heart to be clear before God and in so much as you are able, you want to be at peace with all men.

# HOW TO BE AN ASSET TO YOUR LOCAL CHURCH AND GOD'S KINGDOM

Did you know that you have the potential to be and do great things? Did you know that through the choices you make, your temporary life can impact eternity? Do you realize what type of blessing and asset you can be to your local church and to the kingdom of God? Your piece in God's big puzzle matters! There are several strategic ways to maximize your life, your influence and your contribution to your local church. There are also few ways to limit your effectiveness. In this chapter, we want to discuss how you can hone and develop your skills to maximize your impact and influence for the Lord in your local church and in God's kingdom.

## A. Develop Your People Skills

The ministry is about people! When you serve God you are serving people! When you are dealing with people you are encountering myriads of personalities, attitudes, experiences and personal agendas, and it is necessary that as a servant of God you know how to deal with people effectively. As one preacher said, "Serving God wouldn't be so hard, if it weren't for people!" The joy and heartache of serving God is directly related to our relationships with people! It's important that you develop your people skills: learn how to be a friend, how to speak well of others, how to handle conflict, how to communicate, how to be interested in others and how to mix with all types of people.

In his final address to the Salvation Army, it is reported that General William Booth stood before his officers and bid them farewell with this one word speech: "Others." And with that he sat down. Serving God is all about "others"! Let's look at this subject.

1.  Ask God For Help To Relate To Others

    2 Chronicles 1:7-12

    God asked Solomon a very powerful question. What did God ask him?

    _____

    What was Solomon's request, particularly verse 10?_____

    _____

    Notice that Solomon wanted God's help to know how to "go out and come in before the people" – he wanted help relating to the people, using wisdom and good judgment.

    What was God's response?_____

2.  Walk In Love Toward Others

    a.  Ephesians 5:1-2

        Who are we supposed to imitate?_____

        How are we supposed to walk?_____

    b.  1 Corinthians 13:1-8

        According to verses 1-3, how valuable is our spirituality, knowledge of the Word or life of faith, if we don't walk in love?

        _____

        How is walking in love described in verses 4-8?

        _____

    c.  Proverbs 18:24

        As you walk in love you will find yourself with many friends.  What type of person has friends?

        _____

3.  Be Interested In Others

    When it comes to success in relationships, this is a big secret!  As many relationship experts have said, "The key to being interesting is to be interested."  If you will show a genuine interest in other people, they will show a genuine interest in you!

    Philippians 2:19-21

    Timothy understood this principle.  What did Paul say about Timothy?

    _____

    What did Paul say about most people?_____

    Are you like Timothy?_____

4.  Speak Well of Others

Love believes the best about others!  As a believer, you must choose to believe in and walk in love toward your leaders and other members of God's family.  As in any family there will be occasional "squabbles" and times where you may be offended.  Whether it was accidental or intentional, our feelings can get hurt by others and we must make up our minds in advance that we will not hold grudges and allow bitterness or unforgiveness to rule our hearts, but we will be quick to let the unconditional love of God flow in forgiveness!   Keep a guard over your mouth when you are tempted to be critical or find fault.

a.   Galatians 5:14-15

What happens to our relationships with others if we do not control our mouths?

_____

b.   Ephesians 4:29-5:2

What should never come out of our mouths?_____

_____

What should come out of our mouths?_____

_____

5.   Avoid Discord and Strife With Others

Did you know God hates discord and strife?  You should hate discord and strife, too!  In a church, if the devil can't destroy it from the outside, he will work to destroy it from the inside by stirring up strife.

a.   Proverbs 6:16-19

What seven things does the Lord hate and abhor?

_____    _____

_____    _____

_____    _____

_____

b.   Proverbs 15:18; 16:28; 17:14; 20:3; 26:17; 28:25; 29:22

In your own words, describe God's view of strife and discord and what you, as a believer, should do when you are tempted to get involved in strife or discord.

_____

_____

c.   Proverbs 26:20-21

Wood is compared to talebearing, gossip and whispering in this proverb. What happens when there is no wood?

_____

What happens to strife when there is no whisperer?_____

In relationships, the place where we will be most tempted is where our mouth is concerned.  We'll be tempted to share our opinions about the leadership or the church in general as "concerns", and the result will be unpleasant for us and for the church.  We may even be tempted to "spiritualize" our negative comments about others by submitting them as "prayer requests".  It is wise to make a decision right now that you will not participate in strife or things that cause division or discord.

6.   Uproot Bitterness and Plant Forgiveness Toward Others

a.   Hebrews 12:14-15

What are we to follow?_____

What happens if we let a root of bitterness stay in our hearts?

_____

b.   Ephesians 4:31

What are we supposed to do with all bitterness and other ungodly attitudes?

_____

c.   Matthew 6:12-15

If we want to be forgiven by God, what are we supposed to do to those who have offended or hurt us?

_____

7.  Don't Be Easily Offended By Others

One of the biggest problems in church is being "offended". It's vital that you learn how to have thick skin and keep a tender heart where your relationships with others are concerned.

a.  Proverbs 18:19

Why do you think this proverb is true?

_____

# B. Develop Your Word Skills

You need a working knowledge of God's Word! It is amazing how many Christians do not know their Bibles. If you were a farmer you would need a good working knowledge of your tools, right? If you were a soldier you would need a good working knowledge of your weaponry, right? If you were an athlete, you would need a good working knowledge of your equipment, right? Well, you are a "farmer, a soldier and an athlete" for the Lord and you need to know your Bible – it is your toolbox, your weaponry and your equipment!

1.  Proverbs 2:1-5

How hungry are you for God's Word? Describe the verbs in this passage and the intensity they imply.

_____

_____

2.  Psalm 119

Read all of Psalm 119 (it's the longest Psalm in the Bible) and describe the passion for God's Word that David described.

_____

_____

3.  2 Timothy 2:15

What are we commanded to do with God's Word?_____

What is the result?_____

4.  Acts 18:24-28

    How is Apollos described?_____

    How did Apollos convince people about Jesus?_____

5.  Colossians 3:16

    What is the Word supposed to do in our hearts?_____

    For what purpose?_____

# C. Develop Your Devotional Life

The art of seeking God, fellowshipping with the Lord and inquiring of Him is a necessity.  Prayer and fellowship with God is your connection to heaven!  We are workers together with God and we need to be in step with Him; only developing our devotional life can do this.

If the truth be known, everything about fruitful service to God comes from the overflow of your prayer and Word life with God.  Devotion, prayer, and spending time in His Word is the absolute foundation to your life in God!  If you need to know what "Headquarters" wants to communicate, you need to pray and seek God!  It is through prayer and spending time with the Lord that we receive direction and encouragement.  A wonderful woman of God once pointed out the difference between our "personal" relationship with the Lord and our "business" relationship with the Lord.  It's important to be comfortable in both realms of talking to God.  Let's look at it.

1.  Mark 3:14

    Jesus set the order for service.  Before we are sent out to serve, what are we to do?

    _____

2.  Matthew 4:10

    What comes first, worship the Lord or serve Him?_____

3.  1 Thessalonians 5:17

    How often are we to pray?_____

4.  Philippians 4:6

    What are we to pray about?_____

5.  James 5:16

What does God promise us if we pray fervently?_____

Let's look at this in the Amplified Bible: "...the earnest (heartfelt, continued) prayer of a righteous man makes tremendous power available [dynamic in it's working]."  (AMP)

# D. Develop Your God-Given Talents

1.  Sharpen The Talents God Has Given You

    a.  Ecclesiastes 10:10

        What should we do with the "tools" God has given us?_____

        What's the difference between "working hard" and "working smart"?

        _____

2.  Use The Gifts You Have

    a.  Exodus 4:2-3

        What did God ask Moses?_____

        What did God tell Moses to do with the thing that was in his hand?

        _____

    b.  2 Kings 4:1-7

        In verse 2, what did Elisha ask the widow woman?_____

        What did Elisha tell the widow woman to do with what she had?

        _____

    c.  Mark 6:38-44

        What did Jesus ask the disciples?_____

        What did Jesus do with what they had?_____

If you will recognize what you have and begin to use it, God will touch it supernaturally and cause it to be a blessing! It's really quite simple. Rather than complaining about the gifts or talents you don't have, begin using the ones you do have and watch God touch your life and use you for His glory!

# E. Develop Your Leadership Skills

Good leaders have a heart after God and many character traits that we have already studied in this book. Let's look at four additional, practical things that will help you with your leadership skills.

1.  Personal Discipline

    a.  1 Corinthians 9:24-27

        If you desire "master" level success/leadership, what must you do?

        _____

    b.  Galatians 5:22-23

        What specific "fruit of the Spirit" has to do with our personal discipline?

        _____

2.  Time Management

    a.  Psalm 90:12

        What are we to do regarding our days/time?_____

    b.  Ephesians 5:15-17

        What are we to do with our time?_____

3.  Organizational Skills

    God is not a God of confusion, chaos and disorganization. Just look at His Creation and you will find incredible order and organization and structure! Study the Word to see how many things God "put in order" and organized in both the Old Testament and New Testament.

    a.  1 Corinthians 14:40

        How does God want things done?_____

4.  Communication Skills

a.  Ephesians 4:29

What style of communication should we have?_____

_____

b.  Proverbs 15:1-2

What will a soft answer do? _____

c.  Proverbs 16:21

As a leader who must communicate with others, what secret does this verse give us?

_____

d.  1 Corinthians 9:16-23

Paul described his communication with various types of hearers.  He made it a point to speak to them on their level and in a relevant way.  How is this practical in your life or ministry?

_____

# F. Application

How well do you know the Word of God?  Do you have a conviction that the Bible is indeed God's Word?  Do you esteem the Word as the standard for your life?  Have you considered setting aside some time to give yourself to the study of the Word?  If you are ready for a big challenge? Willing to discipline yourself in th study of God's Word? I want to encourage you to take several months to study this "Expert in the Word" outline and you will be richly blessed.  Support each of your answers with Scripture references.

Expert in the Word Outline

1.  The Doctrine Of The Scriptures.

a.  Can you name ALL the books of the Bible?  If so, do it!
b.  Name 10 of the most significant events in the Old Testament.
c.  What is the longest Psalm and what is it about?
d.  Write a two-sentence summary of each book of the Bible.
e.  What does the Bible being "inspired" mean?
f.  What original languages was the Bible written in?

2.  The Doctrine Of God.

    a.  Give three Scriptures that present the Godhead/Trinity doctrine.
    b.  List 20 attributes of each person of the Godhead – Father, Son, Holy Spirit – and the Scripture references.

3.  The Doctrine Of Man.

    a.  Describe the three-fold nature of man and the Scripture references.
    b.  Describe the creation/commission of man found in Genesis 1 and 2.

4.  The Doctrine Of Sin.

    a.  Describe the fall of man in Genesis 3.  What happened exactly?
    b.  Give three Bible verses that define what sin is.

5.  The Doctrine Of Salvation.

    a.  What is salvation?  Define it.
    b.  Give a Bible argument supporting salvation by faith, not works.

6.  The Doctrine Of The Holy Spirit.

    a.  Who is the Holy Spirit according to John 14-16?
    b.  What does being filled with the Spirit enable us to do according to Acts 1:8?
    c.  What are we commanded in Ephesians 5:18?
    d.  List 5 Bible references to define the difference between being 'born of' and 'filled with' the Spirit?
    e.  List the fruit of the Spirit as found in Galatians 5.

7.  The Doctrine Of The Church.

    a.  Describe the difference between the universal and the local church.
    b.  Who has God called to be officers/ministers in the Church?
    c.  List 10 metaphors used to describe the Church.
    d.  What is the mission of the Church?

8.  The Doctrine Of Angels.

    a.  Describe what you know about angels.  Scriptures?
    b.  Describe what you know about demons.  Scriptures?
    c.  Give five Scriptures that describe the devil, his fall and his defeat.
    d.  Give five Scriptures describing the authority of the believer.

9.  The Doctrine Of Last Things.

    a.  What is the second death according to Revelation 22?
    b.  What happens to those who die before Jesus comes?  Scriptures?
    c.  Give 10 Bible references that talk about end time events other than Revelation.
    d.  What's the difference between the Judgment Seat of Christ and Great White Throne judgment?

10. Basic Doctrines.

    a.  Faith:  Give 10 Scriptures describing the importance of faith.
    b.  Prayer:  Give 10 Scriptures describing how to pray effectively.
    c.  Study:  Give 10 Scriptures describing the need to study the Word.
    d.  Finances:  Give 10 Scriptures describing the believer's relationship to money.
    e.  Well Being:  Give 10 Scriptures describing God's plan for our health/wellness.
    f.  Evangelism:  Give 10 Scriptures describing God's plan for outreach, witnessing and evangelism.

# HOW TO HAVE HEALTHY RELATIONSHIPS BETWEEN LEADERS AND FOLLOWERS

God is relational! His highest and best plan is that there are good relationships between pastors, church and ministry leaders and followers. When you have interpersonal relationships, you have the potential for heartfelt bonds, intimate relationships, great blessing and joy. At the same time, relationships also provide opportunities for offenses, misunderstandings, hurt feelings and rifts, which can even lead to hurting sheep, bitter pastors and church splits. This is not God's will. Let's look at some important keys for cultivating good relationships.

## A. Tips For Having Good Relations Between Leaders And Followers

1. 1 Chronicles 12:1-2,17-18,22,33,38

   In this passage we see the heart relation between God's chosen man, David, and those called to follow him.

   Describe the heart and attitude of submission in these verses.

   _____

   Notice that it was important to David that his followers' hearts were with him. David didn't just want people who were "rah-rah" for the cause. He wanted people who had him in their hearts. This is important. While all leaders and followers should have Jesus first and foremost in their hearts, it is biblical to have a healthy allegiance to the leader you are following. It is also appropriate for the leader to have the followers in his or her heart as well. We see this demonstrated in David's life as well as the Apostle Paul's life and ministry. God's kingdom and spiritual issues are matters of the heart and must be done from the heart!

2. 1 Corinthians 11:1

   How are we to follow those that lead us?_____

3. Philippians 1:3-7

   Describe Paul's heart toward those who followed him._____

4. 1 Thessalonians 2:1-13; 5:12-13

   What type of relationship is described between leaders and followers in these passages?

In a small church it is very possible that you may personally know the pastor and his family and/or the staff on a first-name basis. Although you may not be having lunch on a weekly basis with the pastor, you may be able to "know" him or her on a more personal level. In a large church it may not always be possible to "know" those over you in the Lord on a personal, first-name basis. The way to "know" those over you in the Lord in a large church is to listen, read and follow the heart and communication that comes from the senior leadership. For example, if your pastor teaches specific classes, or has audio or video messages, an online presence or has written a blog or books, it is wise to follow, listen and read those things to "get to know those over you in the Lord." It is also wise to get involved in an area of ministry and know those leaders who have been given spiritual authority in a department.

## B. 10 Things Every Pastor Wants Their Church Members To Know

1.  Your Pastor Wants You To Have A Devotional Life With God

As a Christian and a fruitful member of the church, it is important that you have your own personal devotional life with the Lord! This includes engaging in regular personal Bible reading and prayer. While God uses the church to minister and confirm His Word to you, the primary way He will speak to your heart is through your personal devotional life.

2.  Your Pastor Wants You To Walk In Love And Build Bridges To Others

Love believes the best about others! As a member, you must choose to believe in, and walk in love toward, the leadership, other members and our guests. Like any family there will be occasional "squabbles" and times where you may be offended. Whether it was accidental or intentional, our feelings can get hurt by others and we must make up our minds in advance that we will not hold grudges or allow bitterness or unforgiveness to rule our hearts, but be quick to let the unconditional love of God flow in forgiveness!

Look for ways to build bridges to other Christians and churches in town: let's not have an exclusive attitude toward those outside our church. If anyone calls on Jesus as Lord, they are our brother and sister, so let's reach out. At the same time, we realize that not every person or every church will agree with every point of doctrine our church stands for. Anyone can be a critic and disagreeable, but as a member, always be on the lookout for ways to build bridges to people! Be a person who walks in wisdom from above by peacefully guarding, protecting and defending the honor of the church, the leadership and others, while at the same time looking for common grounds of agreement. If you are persecuted or hear unfounded criticisms of the church from others, in love, give a reasonable defense and endeavor to be a peacemaker and a bridge builder!

3.  Your Pastor Wants You To Find A Place To Serve

As a member, it is important that you are supportive of and involved in the vision, plans and programs the church offers. Nothing stops the momentum or hurts a church more than people who are out of "alignmenet" with the vision, mission and direction the pastor is taking the church. It is much easier to accomplish God's plans and purposes when the majority of the congregation has their foot on the "gas" rather than on the "brakes"! Don't be a "wet-blanket, stick-in-the-mud, pew warmer": be an active and enthusiastic encourager and a supporter of the vision! As a member, you need to be involved serving in the church in some capacity, whether in an area of helps like welcome ministry, parking lot, ushers, children's ministry, youth, praise team, small groups, outreach or other areas of ministry! There are always openings for you to begin serving and let your "gift" make a way for you.

4.  Your Pastor Wants You To Participate In The Life Of The Church

Pastors and leaders count on members to actively participate in the life of the church. The reason for this isn't so that your name can be counted in the attendance figure, it's because the various services, special events, classes, small groups and ministries are specifically designed to meet your needs. At the same time, we understand that you have a life outside the church and we don't expect you to be there every time the doors open, but we do expect members to attend more than just on Sunday mornings.

5.  Your Pastor Wants You To Pray For One Another

One of the best things you can do for the leadership of the church, for other members and attenders, and for members of our community is to pray for them! God hears and answers prayer, and as members of the same church, a local example of His Body, we need to cover one another in prayer. For starters, pray the prayers in Ephesians 1:16-20 and Colossians 1:9-11 for us leaders and church members.

6.  Your Pastor Wants You To Be A Good Witness For Christ

Jesus gave us the Great Commission to "Go ye into all the world and preach the gospel..." Church members should be committed to sharing the gospel through their lifestyle, friendships, words and deeds. Jesus will make us fishers of men as we follow Him! Not only are you called to be a witness for Christ, but as a church member, people will be watching your personal lifestyle to see what "those Christians" are really like! The world is looking for hypocrites in the church, so let your life prove the genuineness of your faith. Let your life preach! Be a person who "talks and walks" the Word of God. Be a person who has the "spirit of faith" about them and who trusts God. Be friendly. Be generous. Be complimentary. Be a person of Christian character and integrity. Let your words edify others. Be an example of what a true Christian is really like!

7.  Your Pastor Wants You To Give Tithes And Offerings

God loves a cheerful giver and so do we! We don't want you to feel manipulated or pressured to give to the church, but we want you to recognize the eternal value of giving to the work of God and to give cheerfully! We want you to understand, obey and experience the benefits of God's promises and the law of sowing and reaping for those who tithe and give offerings. Church members are expected to tithe and are encouraged to give offerings as needs are presented. Through the faithful giving of those who tithe and give offerings, a church is blessed and able to be a blessing to others. Jesus said, "...where your heart is, there will be your treasure also."

8.  Your Pastor Wants You To Guard Your Tongue

The Bible says that no man can tame the tongue, but God can! If anything gives us trouble, it's usually our mouth! In the church world, it seems that our tongues require the most discipline. Don't be deceived into becoming an opinion-ated gossip, backbiter, divider or whisperer. Let no unwholesome word proceed from your mouth, but only things that edify others! At times, you may not understand or agree with a decision the leadership has made. Fortunately, you will not be held accountable for the decision, but you will be held accountable for the way you handle your opinion and your words. Keep a guard over your mouth when you are tempted to be critical or find fault. If the enemy cannot destroy a church from the outside, he will seek to destroy it from the inside through strife and discord. It's no wonder the Bible says, God hates the sowing of discord among the church family.

These days, with the popularity of social media (Facebook, Twitter, Instagram, etc.), it's even more important that you walk in love and exercise self-control when you are tempted to become offended, critical or judgmental. Posting negative comments, condescending opinions or sharing "dirty laundry" on the internet is not only a bad witness for Christ, it's destructive to the chuch—and God doesn't like it.

9.   Your Pastor Wants You To Understand His/Her Calling

Pastors are human, just like you. While it is a great honor and an overwhelming assignment to be given the privilege of leading God's people, we recognize our own human inability and weakness. However, we are confident that as we receive His grace, through faith, we can do all things through Christ who strengthens us. We recognize His anointing in our lives to serve you in ministry, and at the same time we must live our everyday life by faith, just like you. We must choose to walk in the light of the Word each day. We must choose to believe God's Word in our heart and to confess it and obey it just as you do. We appreciate your overlooking our human flaws and trusting God to use us in your life. We would never demand your respect or honor, but we know the blessings that would come into your life if you would choose to esteem and honor our role in your life as one called by God to lead and feed you spiritually.

Our family life is a work in progress. We have a blessed marriage, but we must work at it just like you. We aren't perfect. Our kids are normal kids, just like yours. Our kids have not memorized the entire Bible and they are not perfect. Like you, we are doing our best to raise them in the nurture and admonition of the Lord, and we are trusting God to mold and shape them as they grow and develop. We appreciate your understanding that.

10.  Your Pastor Wants You To Understand His/Her Heart

As a Pastor or church leader, we love the sheep and will do our best to feed and lead. We know our responsibility to feed you God's Word, to lead by example and to protect you from people, doctrine and things that do not have your best interest in mind. We realize our responsibility to give ourselves to prayer and the ministry of the Word, to see that the needs of the sheep are cared for, and to train and equip God's people for the work of the ministry. We have your best interest in mind and by God's grace we will fulfill His calling on our lives for your benefit.

# C. 10 Things Every Church Member Wants Their Pastor To Know

1.   Your Member Wants You To Keep Your First Love For The Lord

As a church member, we want to know that your first love is the Lord. We want to have the confidence that you are spending time with the Lord, spending time in the Word and prayer and that you are maintaining a close fellowship with Jesus – the Head of the Church. Your walk with the Lord gives us great confidence and comfort as we follow you and God's plan for our church.

2.  Your Member Wants You To Share Your Purpose And Vision

We want to hook up with your purpose and vision. We need to know precisely what the purpose and vision is! What has God put in your heart? What is the purpose, vision, mission and strategy of our church? It would help us to see it written down so that we could run with you as we fulfill God's will. (Habakkuk 2:2) When the purpose and vision is blurry to us, it is difficult for us to engage our hearts.

3.  Your Member Wants You To Be Friendly

We appreciate your smiles, your hello's and occasional notes. We realize that you have many internal and external demands on your time, mind, emotions and strength, and yet, it still means alot to us when you take time to to extend your love. Your friendly smile and comments mean a lot to us.

4.  Your Member Wants To Be Appreciated

We know that we are serving the Lord and not men, but it sure is nice to be appreciated once in a while. When you mention your thankfulness to or about anyone in the congregation, it makes all of us feel appreciated. We will serve the Lord whether we receive appreciation or not, but your words of honor and appreciation does encourage us in our service to the Lord.

5.  Your Member Wants You To Remember They Have A Job And Family Life

We have a busy life, just like you! We work in high paced, stress-filled jobs, many times in an environment that is not Christian in nature and that is sometimes unpleasant. We are busy raising our families, running kids to sports, school and church events, maintaining a home and paying our bills. We love to serve God by participating in the life of the church, and yet from time to time, we need to moderate and balance our schedules for the benefit of our personal lives and family health, and in order to be more effective in our service to the Lord. Thanks for understanding this.

6.  Your Member Wants You To Preach The Word, Not Personal Convictions

We love it when you preach the Word! The Word of God feeds us. We are hungry for the Word and we trust you to feed us good doctrine and practical applications from the Bible. We feel uncomfortable when you get on your "soapbox" and begin to preach your personal convictions as something each of us must adopt. We respect you greatly, and many of your personal convictions are ours as well, but when the Word convinces us rather than your intellect or emotional pull, it takes much better root in our hearts.

7.  Your Member Wants You To Be An Example

We know you are not perfect, but we do look to you as an example. We do watch you. We watch and listen to your walk with God. We do watch you and your spouse, and your kids, and we are looking for genuine people who really live the Christian life. We don't want you to feel pressured to be something you are not, to be phony or to put on a "church-face" for us; we just want to observe your Christian life in action. We appreciate it when we observe you interacting with people, using gracious words, making sacrifices and taking actions that demonstrate your humility and servant heartedness. We appreciate your stand of faith and how you practice what you preach by fighting the fight of faith when you face trials, rather than telling us each week of the woes you are facing. We see your example of a person who trusts God in his/her life and this is a model we are watching.

8.    Your Member Wants You To Avoid Using Pressure, Guilt or Manipulation

We are not looking for someone to control us. We are looking for someone to lead us. Pressure, guilt, gimmicks and manipulation tactics may work for a while when it comes to receiving the offering, recruiting church workers or encouraging church attendance, but in the long run we will tire of it and look for a place where leadership is done in love and by the Word.

9.    Your Member Wants You To Know They Have A Heart To Help You

We want to help. God has put a desire and unique gifts in our hearts to help you and the vision God has given you. We are willing and eager; we just need to know how! It would be helpful if you could let us know the "steps" or process by which we can get involved in an area of ministry. It would help us to understand the organization or protocols of the church so that we are a support and a blessing to you, your staff and key leaders when it comes to our church involvement. We also realize that as the church grows, the responsibilities, oversight and time demands of the Senior Leadership increase as well, and while our personal contact with you may be limited, we want to help by being a part of the growing team of leaders and helpers that God is adding to this church.

10.    Your Member Wants You To Know Their Heart

We love the Lord. We love His Word. We love our Pastor and church family! We are committed to God's kingdom. Thank you for seeing our hearts and understanding and caring about our lives.

## D. Application

This might be a good time to write a note of thanks and appreciation!

If you are a Pastor or leader, it might be nice to write individual notes as you are able, or a letter to your entire congregation or ministry departments expressing the love, thanks and appreciation that is in your heart for them and their support and help.

If you are church member, this might be a good time for writing a note of appreciation to your pastor or other church leaders you esteem. Remember that your words can literally "minister grace to the hearers" according to Ephesians 4:29.

# HOW TO KEEP
# THE MAIN THING THE MAIN THING

Jesus never lost sight of His purpose, and neither should we! It's vital that we keep the main thing the main thing! We can get so busy keeping the "ministry machine" operating that we forget why we are doing ministry to begin with! Let's conclude this study by refreshing our hearts and minds to the main thing!

## A. Never Forget The Great Commission

1.  Matthew 28:18-20, Mark 16:15-20

    What were Jesus' last words, also known as the Great Commission?

    _____

    GOSPEL: The Gospel of Jesus Christ is good news. Gospel means good news. The good news is that although we were slaves of sin, doomed to eternal death and subject to sickness and poverty, Jesus Christ through His death on the cross, His shed blood, His burial and resurrection has once and for all released mankind from the bondage of sin, sickness and poverty. The good news of the Gospel is that through Jesus Christ we can be reconciled with our loving heavenly Father. This is called the "Great Commission." Every believer has been commissioned by Jesus to go into their world to tell others the good news of salvation through faith in Jesus Christ.

2.  2 Corinthians 5:17-21

    What ministry has God called every believer to be involved in? _____

    _____

    We are called "_____ for _____"

    In your own words, how would you define an "ambassador"? _____

    _____

3.  Romans 10:13-15

    Who can be saved? _____

    Before a person can call on the Lord, he must _____

Before a person can believe in Jesus, he must _____

Before a person hears about Christ, there must be a _____

Will you allow God to use you to be a preacher of the Good News?_____

4.  Acts 1:8

When the Holy Spirit comes upon us we receive power to do what?

_____

In your own words, how would you define a witness?_____

_____

5.  1 Corinthians 9:19-23

Who are we to serve? (v. 19)_____

What is Paul describing in verses 20-22?_____

_____

In order to relate to sinners and "become all things to all men", do we need to participate in ungodly practices?

_____

How do we go into all the world and befriend unbelievers, becoming all things to all men, and yet maintain a lifestyle pleasing to God (being in the world but not of the world,  John 17:16)?  In your own life, how do you do this?

_____

6.  Luke 15:1-7

Who came to hear Jesus?  (vv. 1,2)_____

Who got mad at Jesus for being with sinners?_____

What was Jesus telling us about the priority of finding the "lost"?

_____

Jesus was a great example of being in the world, but not of it.  He knew how to be a friend to sinners without condemning them; at the same time, He was not dragged into their sin and hypocrisy.

7.  Proverbs 11:30

What does a wise person do?_____

Every believer has been given the commission to go into all the world and preach the Gospel and to make disciples of all nations.  There are lost people all around us.  Pray and ask God which of the unsaved people you come in contact with each day you should befriend and begin sharing the good news of Jesus Christ with.

## B. Never Forget The Great Commandment

Living by the "law of love" is the bottom line to real Christianity.  Let's look at it.

1.  Matthew 22:36-40

What is the Great Commandment?_____

What two commands make up the one Great Commandment?

_____    _____

2.  1 Corinthians 13:1-8

If we can speak in tongues, but do not walk in love, what are we?

_____

If we prophesy and have revelation knowledge, but don't walk in love, what are we?

_____

If we have mountain-moving faith, but do not walk in love, what are we?

_____

If we give all we own to the poor, but do not walk in love, what are we?

_____

If we lay down our lives and are burned, but do not walk in love, what do we have?

_____

Notice that speaking in tongues, prophecy, faith, giving to the poor and laying down your life as a martyr are apparently all wonderful, desirable Christian attributes, but to walk in love supercedes them all.

Describe the kind of love this passage is talking about.  Think about how it would apply in your relationships with others – your spouse, your children, your employer, your employees, your friends, your pastor, your fellow Christians, other churches, other races and even your enemies.

_____

_____

3.    John 13:34,35; 15:12-17, James 2:8, Romans 13:8-10

Notice how important this command is, and paraphrase these verses in your own words.

_____

_____

4.    1 John 3:14-24;  4:7-8,10-12

The Apostle John had a lot to say about our love walk.  Paraphrase these verses in your own words, and consider how they apply to the relationships in your life right now.

_____

Living by the Great Commandment is a great joy and also a great challenge at times.  When we choose to believe the best about others and when we choose to say good things about others, we will experience His joy and be blessed. In our church relationships this is important, because many times the enemy uses those closest to us to hurt us the most – whether it was accidental or intentional – and we must choose love.  In our relationships with other churches in our community, we must realize that we are not competing with other churches, but we are to compliment them and work together to minister to our communities.  It is important to guard your heart and your words as it relates to other churches.  While we may disagree on some minor doctrinal points, we are still one Body of Christ. We can disagree without being disagreeable – we can walk in love!

## C. Never Forget We Are To Live By Great Faith

Faith is what pleases God!  Faith in God and His Word is expected for each and every Christian.  Everything we do for God and everything we receive from God will be done by faith.  We must live by faith.  Living by faith is not an option for a Christian: it is a command.  If you study Jesus' life, you'll notice that He did not have any tolerance for doubt and unbelief. He consistently rebuked, challenged and questioned those who had "little faith", "doubt" or "weak faith".  He often said things like, "You of little faith, why did you doubt?" and "Where is your faith?" Jesus expects us to believe God and His Word and He does not wink at unbelief.  We have a responsibility to know what God's Word says and to believe it, speak it and act as if it were so.  Can you see room for growth in your faith life?  Good news!  God has given us the secret for growing and obtaining more faith!  Let's look at this subject.

1.   Luke 7:1-9

What did Jesus commend the Centurion for?_____

Why do you think Jesus considered the words the Centurion spoke to be a demonstration of great faith?

_____

Isn't it interesting that Jesus defined "great faith" as simply accepting the authority of His Word?  Taking God at His Word, and banking your life on the fact that God will back His own Word is great faith in action.  Jesus likes it!

2.   Romans 1:17, Galatians 3:11

What are believers to live by?_____

3.   2 Corinthians 5:7

We walk by _____ NOT by _____

4.   2 Corinthians 4:13

To live by faith, or to have the spirit of faith, we must believe something in our hearts and we must speak something with our mouths.  What does this verse tell us?

_____

5.   Hebrews 11:6

What must we have in order to please God?_____

Do you know why it takes faith to please God?  It's not because God is a "hard-to-please" ogre.  It's because God knows that faith is the vehicle He has given us for obtaining things from Him, for experiencing what is impossible with man and for walking in all the blessings He has promised in His Word.  It takes faith to receive from God.  When we receive all God has provided, it pleases Him!  Just like any good father delights to see his children blessed, God our Father is pleased when we walk by faith and experience His goodness.

6.   Luke 18:8

When Jesus comes again, what will He be looking for?_____

7.  Hebrews 11:1,3

    What is faith?  Give an example of how God operates in faith?_____

8.  Romans 10:17

    How do we get more faith?_____

Your faith can grow!  God wants your faith to increase and He has told us just exactly how to get more faith.  Faith comes as you spend time in the Word.  The more time you spend in the Word and the more you hear God's Word, the more faith will come!  It's quite simple.  Faith comes from feeding on God's Word.

Faith is such an important subject; it is worth your time to study this subject in more detail so that you will understand the law of faith God has instituted.  Because there have been many zealous yet misguided Christians in the area of faith who failed to get the whole picture before they ran off into faith adventures that crashed and burned, we encourage you to take some time in God's Word to get a well-rounded and comprehensive understanding of this subject!  Locate yourself and begin to feed your faith so that Jesus can marvel at your faith and it can be said of you, "You, the just, have lived by faith."

# D. Application

Are you living by Great Faith?  Living for the Great Commission?  Living out the Great Commandment?  Let's focus on the Great Commission for a moment.

Do you have unsaved family members or friends?  Do you work with or live near anyone that does not know the Lord?  Does your heart seem to go toward any one of them in particular?  I want to encourage you to begin praying for those that don't know Jesus and seek God for an opportunity to share the gospel with them.
Here are four ways you can pray for those who are unsaved.

1.  **Pray For Their Eyes To be Opened**

    2 Corinthians 4:4, Ephesians 1:17-18, Luke 24:31-32,  Acts 26:16

2.  **Pray For Jesus-Loving, Gospel-Preaching Laborers To Be Sent To Them**

    Matthew 9:36-39, Isaiah 6:8, John 6:44, John 12:32

3.  **Pray For God's Grace To Be Received By Them**

    Ephesians 2:8, Hebrews 4:16, Titus 2:11

4.  **Pray For Them To Have A Heart To Repent**

    Romans 2:4, 2 Corinthians 7:9-10, 2 Peter 3:9, 1 John 5:14-15

# ABOUT THE AUTHOR

Beth Jones has been helping people 'get the basics' of God's Word for over thirty years. She is the author of over twenty books, including the popular Getting A Grip On The Basics Bible study series being used by thousands of churches in America and abroad. She hosts The Basics With Beth TV program aired around the world and she and her husband Jeff founded and serve as the senior pastors of Valley Family Church in Kalamazoo, Michigan.

**For more resources from Beth or to contact her ministry, just go to:**

**thebasicswithbeth.com**

Made in United States
Troutdale, OR
01/08/2025

27741521R00058